Unlocking the Master Narrative

Bassim Hamadeh, CEO and Publisher
Kristina Stolte, Acquisitions Editor
Tim Pike, Project Editor
Berenice Quirino, Associate Production Editor
Miguel Macias, Senior Graphic Designer
Sara Schennum, Licensing Associate
Natalie Piccotti, Director of Marketing
Kassie Graves, Vice President of Editorial
Jamie Giganti, Director of Academic Publishing

Cover copyright©
Source: https://commons.wikimedia.org/wiki/File:Chief_Joseph_of_the_Nez_Perces.jpg
Source: https://commons.wikimedia.org/wiki/File:Motto_web_dubois_original.jpg
Source: https://commons.wikimedia.org/wiki/File:Emiliano_Zapata-Libreria_del_Congreso.jpg
Source: https://commons.wikimedia.org/wiki/File:Chinese_work_crew_VPL_66958_
(10985351363).jpg
Source: https://en.wikipedia.org/wiki/File:John_F._Kennedy,_White_House_photo_portrait,_
looking_up.jpg
Source: https://commons.wikimedia.org/wiki/File:Tents_at_Camp_4_of_the_Copper_Riv-
er_and_Northwestern_Railway_showing_workers_loading_freight_onto_a_flatbed_railroad_
car,_April_(HEGG_761).jpeg

Printed in the United States of America.

ISBN: 978-1-5165-3890-4 (pbk) / 978-1-5165-3891-1(br)

Unlocking the Master Narrative

History and Intercultural Communication

First Edition

Scott M. Finnie and Angela Davis Wizner

 cognella® | ACADEMIC PUBLISHING

Table of Contents

Preface

Plurality is a double-edged sword,
where blessing and curse interplay.

Rationale

As a means of background, this book emerged from 12 years
of team teaching American history and intercultural communication. The course, The Changing Face of Discrimination,
laid the foundation for the direction of this text. With emphasis
on domestic intercultural communication and America's growth
as a nation-state, our scope of treatment is intentionally limited
and succinct in nature.

Research combining these two fields of study was generally
scant and underdeveloped, especially dealing with our theme
regarding the Master Narrative. Thus, the following chapters attempt to address the instrumentality of history and intercultural
communication to afford a new and practical lens for our readers.

Authors

Professor Scott M. Finnie, PhD, is director of the Africana Studies Program at Eastern Washington University in Cheney, Washington, and has published numerous articles in the arena of civil rights and African American history.

Professor Angela Davis Wizner, MA, is an educator in the Department of Communication Studies at Spokane Community College in Spokane, Washington, and has 30 years of experience as an author, trainer, and activist in social justice issues.

1 | The Master Narrative and the Collision Theory

An Introduction

The Master Narrative and the Collision Theory

Why do we communicate the way we do? A wide range of variables and factors come into play when analyzing communication styles. Our history, our culture, and our worldview are a few that shape the way we share information with one another. Looking back at these historical roots provides a unique lens into our communication patterns.

Throughout the following chapters, we will take a glimpse at the historical past through the lens of the *MASTER NARRATIVE*, the assumptive legitimization of what is "American." Against this backdrop, we will explore the interplay of history and intercultural communication, which we have defined as *COLLISION*. Why the word *collision*? Our working definition of this concept will be borrowed from the themes found in physics:

> The meeting of bodies in which each exerts a force upon the other, causing the exchange of energy or momentum.

History and intercultural communication, as "bodies" exerting a "force upon the other" (and thus melded together) create an "exchange of energy or momentum" that forms into a master key—that is, a "master key" to "unlock" the Master Narrative as it collides with the co-cultures cited in this text. The end result, we propose, is an "energy or momentum" that provides us a future lens for understanding each other more deeply from a unique perspective.

We will attempt to examine intercultural communication styles throughout this book, specifically styles present in the United States. Looking at these co-cultures and their historic roots, we can better understand perceptual differences in communication interaction by applying this collision theory. Through the definitive lens of the combined methodologies, history, and intercultural communication, actual or potential remedies will be considered based on the impact of communication upon specific historical events.

HISTORY ◄────────────────► INTERCULTURAL COMMUNICATION

History and Communication: *Defined*

Communication is the exchange of information between people working to reach an understanding. The sender encodes a message with the intention of the receiver decoding it correctly. To be successful in the interaction, the sender becomes a decoder as well, and the receiver an encoder. Understanding each other's intent is essential to understanding one another. The challenge is enormous, due to the many variables that come into play when interacting.

Intercultural communication has the same goal as the broad communication definition—to reach understanding. Adding the cultural dimension when examining the interaction provides us a deeper look into why people express themselves as they do. Intercultural communication explores individuals' or groups' shared symbols, language patterns, and belief systems as they interact with others from a different set of variables.

History, on the other hand, is defined as the examination of individual and collective human thought, behavior, and interaction with their legacies. Especially with regards to the dimensions of human interchange historically, intercultural communication broadens the depth of grasping the complexities of historic interpretation.

"E Pluribus Unum": A Pluralistic Society?

As we consider this stage of the American play, pluralism is a fundamental foundation for understanding. As the map reveals, our nation has numerous co-cultures that are rich in history and traditions. With countless ethnicities making up America, this text will emphasize the groups that specifically played an early role as the nation developed in its initial phases. While the indigenous peoples and the Mexicans were already established occupants of the continent, the other three groups were brought here by either compulsion or economic forces.

As seen in the map, the stories of the indigenous peoples, African Americans, Caucasians, Mexican Americans, and Chinese Americans have all been funneled into and filtered through the Master Narrative. The overriding of the lived experiences and perspectives of those outside that of the Master Narrative "norm" is equated in this book to a "locking in" process that can only be remedied by "unlocking" it through the "collision" of history and intercultural communication.

How to Use This Book: A Newly Forged Tapestry

As we study U.S. history and intercultural communication, we will take a unique approach by examining the noted co-cultures within

the United States. As you read through the following chapters, specific themes within these co-cultures will be presented. We will start each examination with the *historic* perspective of each group's experiences and struggles. Following their historic journey, we will see the role of communication and the patterns that emerged during these historic times. By examining the **verbal, nonverbal,** and **cultural** dimensions with **history** (Collision Model), a renewed perception will emerge. Forthcoming, key concepts and theories will be presented to guide you through the chapters ahead.

Historic Timeline: A U.S. Co-culture Overview

The historic unfolding of what is called today the "continental United States" is a tale of arrivals by various people motivated by a myriad of driving forces. The "first Americans," the **indigenous people** of our nation today, arrived thousands of years prior to other groups, coming from upper Mongolia in northern Asia. As they filtered down through today's northern Canada and gradually migrated through North, Central, and South America, their settled presence in what are now the 48 contiguous US states is where we begin our focus. With a constituency of over 500 nations or tribes throughout the Western Hemisphere, the richness and depth of today's indigenous culture is only a remnant of what their ancestors have blessed this part of the world with.

At the time of the first colonial settlement by Britain in 1607, at Jamestown, Virginia, the indigenous population of the United States-to-be was anywhere from 2.5 to 3 million. The next player to come onto the American stage, the founders and purveyors of the Master Narrative, were **the English** who settled along the Eastern

Seaboard on the Atlantic at Virginia, solely as a business venture and enterprise. Twelve years later, to the north, the Plymouth settlement was founded in Massachusetts in 1620 on the basis of religious freedom and autonomy.

But just prior to the landing at Plymouth Rock by the Pilgrims, in 1619 the first persons of **African descent** arrived at Jamestown, Virginia. Brought here forcibly by a Dutch frigate that had intercepted a slave ship on the way to the Caribbean, these initial Africans were not slaves in their newfound American status, but rather were indentured servants. Records indicate that slavery as an institution of lifetime bondage did not commence under British rule until 1640 in the colonies of both Virginia and Maryland. Following the impact of the Revolutionary War (1775–1781) and American independence from England, the new 13 states transitioned from the Articles of Confederation to the U.S. Constitution (1789). In the aftermath of the War of 1812 with England, the Missouri Compromise of 1820 delineated the South from the North with regards to slave and free states, marking a political coexistence with a color-based, dehumanizing institution.

It was also during this decade that waves of economically deprived **immigrant Caucasians** began to arrive by the tens of thousands seeking employment, only to become the North's version of "slaves" as they labored in factories under harsh, discriminatory practices on the part of their employers.

At the close of the next decade, the tragic American Indian death march (referred to as the 1838 Trail of Tears) took place as a message of national and political endorsement. In 1846 the U.S.–Mexican War was initiated by the U.S. military, thus snatching the region of northern Mexico for the renaming of the "American Southwest." This was the start of the **Mexican** being seen as an alien and thus a "stranger in his own land."

Following the Civil War (1861–1865), as American industrialization reached new heights, the 1869 completion of the transcontinental railroad finished off the manipulation of **Chinese labor**, which had been initiated by the 1849 Gold Rush and the mining industry. Thus, the five key players destined to collide with the enforcers of the Master Narrative—*the indigenous peoples, African Americans, Caucasian immigrants, Mexicans and Mexican Americans, and*

Chinese Americans—were all on the same American stage seeking self-determination and self-identity against all odds.

On the following page is a brief timeline that reflects a number of important dates regarding the six players mentioned above, now occupying the same American stage.

Historic Timeline: U.S. Co-culture Overview

1607	Jamestown established in indigenous lands
1619	First 20 Africans brought to Jamestown
1620	Pilgrims arrive at Plymouth Rock
1640	African slavery becomes law in Virginia and Maryland
1775	American Revolutionary War begins
1787	U.S. Constitutional Convention Commences
1815	End of the War of 1812 with Britain
1820	The Missouri Compromise and the great influx of European immigration starts
1838	The tragedy of the Trail of Tears
1846	U.S.–Mexican War
1857	The *Dred Scott* Supreme Court Decision
1861	Start of the American Civil War
1869	Completion of the transcontinental railroad
1877	The collapse of Reconstruction
1896	*Plessy v. Ferguson* Supreme Court decision

Intercultural Communication: Laying the Foundation

Applying the Collision Model, we will examine the *verbal* characteristics of co-cultures and a brief look at their unique language patterns. Not only will we provide information on the spoken word, but also whether they are high- or low-context communicators. A *high-context* communicator is implicit, emphasizing the meaning of the message contextually and in a nonverbal way. Saving the receivers "face" is essential in a successful interaction. *Low-context* communicators have a different lens. They are explicit, sender-centered communicators. The message is in the verbal exchange, and saving the "face" of oneself, rather than the other, is paramount. Many co-cultures have a mix of both, as we will see in the chapters ahead.

Our **nonverbal** review of co-cultures looks at how we communicate beyond the verbal dimension. *Messages sent using other than linguistic means* can be quite powerful. Researchers found that nonverbal communication makes up much of our conversation, up to 93% of the message. To examine the U.S. co-cultures and their use of nonverbal communication, the following dimensions will be explored.

Dimensions of Nonverbal Communication

Proxemics: humans' use of space
Oculesics: humans' use of eyes; eye contact
Haptics: humans' use of touch
Olfaltrics: humans' use of smell
Chronemics: humans' use of time
Kinesics: humans' use of body movement; outer self

Source. Adapted from Hall (1966).

Culture, the last variable to consider, examines unique patterns belonging only to the co-culture being reviewed. Hofstede's dimensions of *cultural variability* provide a picture of these patterns. Coupling these patterns will be a brief look at the co-cultures' *worldview,* including their religious and philosophical perspectives. In addition, the *Pyramid of Failed Communication* provides an examination of the effects discrimination has on the communication process.

Anthropologist Geert Hofstede categorized world cultures based on several cultural variables he observed. We will be specifically applying four of his categories listed above for our analysis of co-cultures within the United States. A chart representing world countries and scores are listed is shown here:

Cultural Orientations: Characteristics

High power distance	Low power distance
• Clear hierarchy established	• Less hierarchy favored
• Unequal power expected	• Equal power is expected
• Status and rank important	• Decision making is shared
• Rigid value system	• Roles are fluid
• Centralized organizational power	• Decentralized organizational structure

Collectivism	Individualism
• Community is emphasized	• Individual is the center of society
• "Face talk" is considered harmonious	• "Straight talk" is valued
• Group/family achievement is honored	• Individual achievement is important
• Cooperation is favored	• Privacy is expected
• Loyalty to one's family and company	• Loyalty to many organizations in one's lifetime is preferred

High uncertainty avoidance	Low uncertainty avoidance
• Ambiguity is uncomfortable	• Ambiguity is comfortable
• Formal roles are necessary	• Less structure is favored
• Differences are discouraged	• Differences are tolerated
• Higher stress levels are present	• Risk taking is more present
• Hierarchical decision making is important	• Decision making is shared

Masculine	Feminine
• Male-oriented society	• Nurturing-oriented society
• Money and things are important	• People and environment are important
• Rights of men and women differ	• Sexual equality is expected
• Competition is respected	• Cooperation is valued
• Task takes precedence over relationships	• Relationships take precedence over task

Source. Adapted from Geert Hofstede, Culture's Consequences: Comparing Values, Behaviors, Institutions and Organizations Across Nations. Copyright © 2001 by SAGE Publications.

TABLE 1.1   Index Values and Rank of 50 Countries and 3 Regions on Four Culture Dimensions

Country	Abbreviation	Power Distance Index (PDI)	Rank	Uncertainty Avoidance Index (UAI)	Rank	Individualism Index (IDV)	Rank	Masculinity Index (MAS)	Rank
Argentina	ARG	49	18–19	86	36–41	46	28–29	56	30–31
Australia	AUL	36	13	51	17	90	49	61	35
Austria	AUT	11	1	70	26–27	55	33	79	49
Belgium	BEL	65	33	94	45–46	75	43	54	29
Brazil	BRA	69	39	76	29–30	38	25	49	25
Canada	CAN	39	15	48	12–13	80	46–47	52	28
Chile	CHL	63	29–30	86	36–41	23	15	28	8
Colombia	COL	67	36	80	31	13	5	64	39–40
*Costa Rica	COS	35	10–12	86	36–41	15	8	21	5–6
Denmark	DEN	18	3	23	3	74	42	16	4
*Equador	EQA	78	43–44	67	24	8	2	63	37–38
Finland	FI	33	8	59	20–21	63	34	26	7
France	FRA	68	37–38	86	36–41	71	40–41	43	17–18
German (F.R.)	GER	35	10–12	65	23	67	36	66	41–42
Great Britain	GBR	35	10–12	35	6–7	89	48	66	41–42
Greece	GRE	60	26–27	112	50	35	22	57	32–33
*Guatemala	GUA	95	48–49	101	48	6	1	37	11
Hong Kong	HOK	68	37–38	29	4–5	25	16	57	32–33
*Indonesia	IDO	78	43–44	48	12–13	14	6–7	46	22
India	IND	77	42	40	9	48	30	56	30–31
Iran	IRA	58	24–25	59	20–21	41	27	43	17–18
Ireland	IRE	28	5	35	6–7	70	39	68	43–44
Israel	ISR	13	2	81	32	54	32	47	23
Italy	ITA	50	20	75	28	76	44	70	46–47
*Jamaica	JAM	45	17	13	2	39	26	68	43–44
Japan	JPN	54	21	92	44	46	28–29	95	50
*Korea (S.)	KOR	60	26–27	85	34–35	18	11	39	13
*Malaysia	MAL	104	50	36	8	26	17	50	26–27
Mexico	MEX	81	45–46	82	33	30	20	69	45
Netherlands	NET	38	14	53	18	80	46–47	14	3
Norway	NOR	31	6–7	50	16	69	38	8	2
New Zealand	NZL	22	4	49	14–15	79	45	58	34
Pakistan	PAK	55	22	70	26–27	14	6–7	50	26–27
*Panama	PAN	95	48–49	86	36–41	11	3	44	19
Peru	PER	64	31–32	87	42	16	9	42	15–16
Philippines	PHI	94	47	44	10	32	21	64	39–40
Portugal	POR	63	29–30	104	49	27	18–19	31	9
South Africa	SAF	49	18–19	49	14–15	65	35	63	37–38
*Salvador	SAL	66	34–35	94	45–46	19	12	40	14
Singapore	SIN	74	40	8	1	20	13–14	48	24
Spain	SPA	57	23	86	36–41	51	31	42	15–16
Sweden	SWE	31	6–7	29	4–5	71	40–41	5	1
Switzerland	SWI	34	9	58	19	68	37	70	46–47
Taiwan	TAI	58	24–25	69	25	17	10	45	20–21
Thailand	THA	64	31–32	64	22	20	13–14	34	10
Turkey	TUR	66	34–35	85	34–35	37	24	45	20–21
*Uruguay	URU	61	28	100	47	36	23	38	12
U.S.A.	USA	40	16	46	11	91	50	62	36
Venezuela	VEN	81	45–46	76	29–30	12	4	73	48
Yugoslavia	YUG	76	41	88	43	27	18–19	21	5–6
Regions:									
*East Africa	EAF	64	(31–32)	52	(17–18)	27	(18–19)	41	(14–15)
*West Africa	WAF	77	(42)	54	(18–19)	20	(13–14)	46	(22)
*Arab Ctrs.		80	(44–45)	68	(24–25)	38	(35)	53	(28–29)

*Based on data added later.

Source: Geert Hofstede, "National Cultures in Four Dimensions: A Research-Based Theory of Cultural Differences among Nations," *International Studies of Management and Organization*, vol. 13, no. 1-2. Copyright © 1983 by Taylor & Francis Group.

Belief Systems

World View	Deities/Key Leaders	Writings	Key Principles
Judaism	Yahweh	Torah in Hebrew Bible	God's chosen people; God is one; no human will ever be divine.
Christianity	God (the Trinity: Father, Son, and Holy Spirit)	Holy Bible	Jesus is the Savior; two greatest commandments are love God and love your neighbor as yourself.
Islam	Allah	Quran	Five Pillars of Practice: fasting, almsgiving, pilgrimage, creed, prayer.
Buddhism	Buddha	Pali Canon	Four Noble Truths; the Eightfold Path; overcoming suffering leads to Nirvana.
Confucianism	Confucius	Analects	Social, political, and ethical concepts inspired by Confucius's teachings.
Hinduism	Brahma, Vishnu, Shiva	Upanishads and the Bhagwat Gita	Divine in every thing; dharma, a way of life; multiple paths.

Note. These represent the six largest worldviews globally.

The *Pyramid of Failed Communication* (opposite page) attempts to identify the connective tissues of inordinate interaction between individuals. As the pyramid shows, *ethnocentrism* is the originating thrust of this communication dysfunction. In light of the Master Narrative, this assumed superiority in the context of American history can also be labeled as Eurocentrism. This base is the first stepping stone to enhanced negative perceptions of individuals. Next is *stereotyping*, in which our automatic assumptions come into play, and those "pictures in our head" become a perceived reality. Our attitude follows this subconscious process and lends itself to *prejudice*, which when acted upon creates an environment of *discrimination*. If uninterrupted,

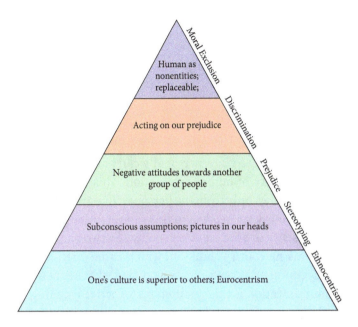

this progression issues a devastating and climactic outcome known as *moral exclusion*. *Moral exclusion*, at the top of the pyramid, is a form of hate that results in the total dismissal of individuals, as they are no longer perceived as human but "expendable and replaceable."

What is forthcoming in the chapters ahead are the distinctive perspectives of the indigenous peoples, African Americans, European American immigrants, Mexican Americans, and Chinese Americans. By affording each group a forum for their own story of lived experiences, we hope to escort the reader to a realm outside of the terms and conditions set forth by the Master Narrative. At such a juncture, the ability and willingness to listen, rather than to simply hear, will be imperative.

Listening stands in sharp contrast to hearing, in spite of commonly held assumptions. Hearing involves a passive receiving of one's story without engaging internally. Listening, on the other hand, demands the dropping of one's perspective to the point that others' lived experiences are subsumed as one's own. This form of intake requires a letting go of one's own "home base" and point of reference under the drive of a newfound willingness to accept others' stories and experiences as valid and authentic. This letting go of such control and privilege inwardly requires a genuine care for others that is projected in the active listening of someone else's "truth." That care, essentially, is an act of mindfulness without any strings attached. The terms and conditions for what is "true" have been transitioned now over to the storyteller.

Once this level of integrity has been individually achieved, the storyteller resonates with a form of validation that heretofore was missing. Being validated interpersonally can have an enormous impact on the integrity of human interaction. This newfound validation, however, comes only from the personal investment of listening. What spontaneously springs out of this type of organic validation is trust. The presence or absence of trust between two parties is dependent upon this newborn validation, which came forth out of true, engaged listening. As a result, we may say that what lies at the root of failed communication is this missing link of active listening.

At such a juncture, a shared historical consciousness has transpired. Such consciousness, now shared and collective, is what can truly "unlock" the Master Narrative while simultaneously administer a healing bond of mutuality, newly found and newly surfaced. This healing bond of mutuality affords what both Malcolm X and Dr. Martin Luther King Jr. referred to as the "beloved community." The Master Narrative and its effects are thus submerged beneath the new stream of a shared, historical consciousness that supersedes the confined and narrow approach to history previously adopted without scrutiny or inquiry.

As a case in point, the healing bond of mutuality born through genuine listening can remedy a bevy of maladies within our society brought on by the most basic forms of prejudice and discrimination. As one considers the basic sources and origin of prejudice and discrimination, there seem to be five elementary points of initiation to examine. Namely, we can identify them as (a) fear, (b) ignorance, (c) cultural myopia, (d) insecurity, and (e) selfishness. If one reflects upon these five basic elements as the springboards to both prejudice (an inward attitude, an inward picture or image) and discrimination (the outward action based on one's prejudice), what potentially surfaces is a corresponding form of remedy or antidote applicable to each one in particular.

Fear is readily counterpoised by *exposure*, where the unfounded assumptions tend to evaporate or at least lose their weight and leverage in one's estimation. Ignorance meets its remedy in *education*, both formal and informal, as a means to eradicate the groundless biases that were typically both unexamined and uniformed.

Cultural myopia (the "nearsightedness" of one's own upbringing and "incubator" of trusted familiarity) can be countered by *immersion* into other cultural settings and environments for a prolonged time, thereby "unearthing" the circumscribed point of reference previously labeled as "standard" or "normal." Insecurity can be answered with a *sense of dignity* that points to the inherent worth of an individual ascribed to all members of humanity at birth, regardless of the so-called attainments and accomplishments accounted for by mere outward assessments and evaluation.

Finally, selfishness is counterpoised by *sacrifice*; a conscious decision and effort by an individual to "break the link" of that behind-closed-doors prejudice is often voiced and left unconfronted unless someone is willing to lose (or "sacrifice") face and challenge the racial or cultural offense as it surfaces (often in the form of jokes and use of vicious words or terms).

As prejudice and discrimination powerfully dominate the narratives of the five ethnic groups to be reviewed in the following chapters, one can readily see the vital need to surface the five remedies or antidotes mentioned above. Each one has the power to transform a passive "hearer" into an active and engaged "listener" resulting in the noted healing bond of mutuality. This healing process of personal transformation is further identified and explained through this book's unveiling the "Collision Model," addressed at the start of this chapter.

The Collision Model marries the disciplines of history and intercultural communication as a newfound lens to ascertain, diagnose, and remedy the previously insurmountable dysfunctions within our pluralistic society, using the backdrop of unlocking the Master Narrative as its primary aim. Our definition of "collision" points to the untapped effectiveness behind the coupling of these two fields of study: "the meeting of bodies in which each exerts a force upon the other causing the exchange of energy or momentum." By illuminating the Collision Model for our readers, the book enables the healing process that can take place within a setting of intercultural communication and that "borders" a shared historical consciousness.

But our historical tendency, as a nation, has been that of failed communication and the fortification of our siloed and soiled perspectives. Consider the two images adjacent and below in light of this context:

Mere images and symbols can start a chain reaction of the five dynamics cited in the pyramid of failed communication. The hijab, which is a traditional Muslim veil, is highlighted in the first picture. This headpiece has created fertile ground for stereotyping based on one's ethnocentric perceptions. Many cases of threats and intimidation have occurred in the United States due to the wearing of this veil. Although an extreme example, the image of Trayvon Martin in a "hoodie" unfolds the story of prejudice and discrimination, culminating in moral exclusion and the death of this young man. In both instances, the Master Narrative was trespassed and thus met with these outcomes of failed communication.

Trayvon Martin (1995–2012)

Selected Bibliography

Adams, M. B. (Ed.). (2007). *Teaching for diversity and social justice* (2nd ed.). New York: Routledge.

Aguirre, J. A. (2010). *American ethnicity: The dynamics and consequences of discrimination* (7th ed.). New York: McGraw-Hill Education.

Azevedo, M. (Ed.). (2005). *Africana studies: A survey of Africa and the African diaspora* (3rd ed.). Durham, NC: Carolina Academic Press.

Barak, G. (2015). *Class, race, gender, and crime: The social realities of justice in America* (3rd ed.). Lanham, MD: Rowan and Littlefield.

Desmond, M. A. (2016). *Race in America* (1st ed.). New York: Norton.

Feagin, J. R. (2012). *Racial and ethnic relations* (9th ed.). Upper Saddle River, NJ: Pearson Education.

Hall, E. T. (1966). *The hidden dimension*. New York: Doubleday.

Hofstede, G. (2001). *Culture's consequences: Comparing values, behaviors, institutions, and organizations across nations*. Thousand Oaks, CA: Sage.

Mehrabian, A. (2007). *Nonverbal communication*. New Brunswick, NJ: Aldine Transaction.

Oakes, J. E. (2017). *Of the people: A history of the United States with sources* (3rd ed.). New York: Oxford University Press.

Credits

2 | The Master Narrative Unveiled

Manifest Destiny

Unlocking the Master Narrative

As generally noted in the previous chapter, the goal of this text is to examine the intercultural communication and historical origins of the dominant culture's impact on our pluralistic society. Special emphasis will be given to the journey of co-cultures in early America accompanied by experiences through their lenses. What results is a powerful picture of the struggle to survive and be self-defined. Only through understanding the history of our people can we better utilize effective intercultural communication patterns that lead to shared understanding of one another. By unlocking what the Master Narrative has normalized, we can clarify the unfolding of history and the development of intercultural communication processes in a more accurate and realistic manner.

The Master Narrative Defined

As portrayed at the beginning of this chapter, Manifest Destiny was the foundational narrative of the westward land takeover by the British Americans. Even though the first Americans, the indigenous peoples, as well as the Americans that we today note as Mexicans, were already situated, settled, and identified with the territory to be imposed upon—such was romanticized as inevitable "westward expansion." The term *Manifest Destiny* was coined by John L. O'Sullivan in 1845 as a means to justify moral exclusion, categorizing these groups as expendable and nonentities. Completely annihilating the perspective of these two groups, this genocidal land grab was put in the context of a divine mandate, which accompanied them from their initial series of embarking from the British Isles. Yet the most glaring paradox laid within their souls: how to resolve the guiding principles of the **Magna Carta of 1215** against such an offending and offensive backdrop created by their own hands?

This monumental document, laying the groundwork for all modern democracies practiced in the free world, became the bedrock of the future U.S. Constitution and Bill of Rights. As seen on page 22, the Bill of Rights (1791), as the first 10 amendments to the U.S. Constitution, at least on paper, seemed to ensure the private liberties of "all" individuals as well as the powers of individual states.

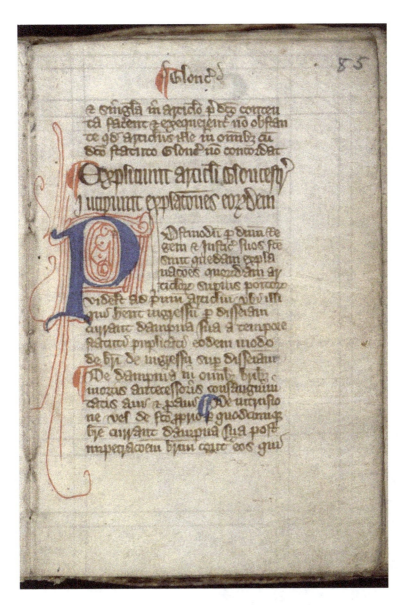

Magna Carta

Bill of Rights (1791)

Yet such profound foundational principles of freedom and rights were paradoxically bestowed only upon landowning, European males. As a result, European females, indigenous populations, as well as newcomers from other parts of the world were all forcibly denied participation in this newly promised society of "true" democracy.

As with all civilizations founded upon conquest and exploitation, the class in control was granted the narrative authority to define what happened as well as the unilateral power to normalize their own cultural peculiarities. Such power to encase one perspective into various forms of generalized sanitation mirrors the system of serfdom within Europe's Dark Ages. Thus, we have what

"To the victor belong the spoils."
New York Senator William L. Marcy,
1832

is termed as the "Master Narrative." The terms and conditions, as a result, for "being American" were forever set in granite by the British colonists and were never to be questioned or scrutinized, especially by those outside this ethnically-defined power class.

The Master Narrative: Its Birth of "Legitimacy"

With the "founding" of the first British colony in North America at Jamestown, Virginia, in 1607, the British enterprise to establish a profitable settlement began. As history tells us, the commercial survival of this enterprise was secured in 1612 with John Rolfe's mastery of tobacco as a primary commodity for trade.

Eight years following the establishment of this economic foothold, the arrival of the Pilgrims from England in 1620 laid forth the religious foundation for the British American colonies' version of protected freedom and individualism. While the early Pilgrims were primarily focused on freedom and spiritual seeking, the latecomers of 1630, known as the Puritans, transformed the Pilgrims' aspirations into a heavy-handed, dominant reli-

gious regiment. This was reinforced and sustained by the profound leadership of John Winthrop, whose famous quote, (adjacent), embodied their mission.

In both centers of commercialism and religious expression, the dominant power group was composed of the European male, whose perspective, traditions, and communication styles became the assumed and expected standard. These individuals came to be identified as WASP (white Anglo–Saxon Protestant), forming the core identity of what was to be "American." Thus, the Master Narrative was brought forth in its initial phase as authentic and undisputed.

"We shall be as a city upon a hill, the eyes of all people are upon us."
John Winthrop, 1630

As the colonies of Britain increased in numbers, the 1600s saw the colonial labor force grow in white indentured servitude accompanied later by the gradual emergence of African enslavement (by 1640). The distinctive class that possessed the colonial power, privilege, and policy making was uniquely confined to white, property-owning males. Among this distinctive group, George Washington rose to the ranks of the continental leadership. As an extremely effective general, he won the general population's confidence unto the birth of a revolution against the lone superpower of the world, England. History tells us that the Declaration of Independence was drawn up with the full backing of at least one third of the colonists ready to bear arms for the cause. This strong commitment for change emerged from a desire for autonomy from the mother country and the odious imposition of

George Washington, General of the Continental Army (1776)

"taxation without representation." It was believed that only under General Washington's leadership could this "miracle" actually be accomplished.

Once independence was secured, the Constitutional Convention of 1787 became the next momentous chapter in the newfound country's history. Again, the 55 delegates that met to produce this noble document of democracy were confined to wealthy, white, landowning males alone.

As a result, the "majority's" perspective as the unquestioned and legitimate truth became normalized, constituting the core of the American status quo. This thematic carryover lasted well into the 1960s, when only the civil rights movement could hold forth both a long-awaited protest and alternative to the Master Narrative.

Historic Timeline: The Master Narrative

1215	The Magna Carta signed
1612	John Rolfe sustains Jamestown's viability via tobacco
1630	Puritan leader John Winthrop initiates "A City Upon a Hill"
1776	American Independence declared
1787	Constitutional Convention at Philadelphia follows Shay's Rebellion
1789	George Washington inaugurated as first president of the United States
1791	The Bill of Rights ratified
1812	War with Britain commences
1828	Andrew Jackson inaugurated seventh U.S. president
1838	The Trail of Tears forced removal
1850	U.S. Congress reaches national compromise over slavery
1860	Abraham Lincoln wins the national election for president
1865	End of Civil War and start of Reconstruction
1883	Civil Rights Act of 1875 ruled unconstitutional by Supreme Court
1896	*Plessy v. Ferguson* makes racial segregation national law

It was at this time that numerous schools of thought were solidified into a series of redefining approaches, models, and paradigms to encapsulate history and the narration of the past, such as Critical Race Theory, liberation ideology, anticolonialism, and Afrocentrism (*The authors of this text highly suggest a dedicated exploration into these noted paradigms for richer, more in-depth clarity*). But as you can see from the previous timeline, following the formation of our nation's constitutional Union, the elusive issue of securing rights for the indigenous population and the African American left one entity intact and deeply embedded in the American psyche: the enforcers of the unscrutinized Master Narrative.

Intercultural Communication and the Master Narrative

The field of intercultural communication examines the interactions between people who have different symbol systems and cultural norms. This definition plays out when examining the Master Narrative and the nondominant cultures within the United States.

Reviewing the dimensions of ethnic groups within American society will provide a foundation for comparing and contrasting the intercultural communication patterns of the different peoples of our nation. We will examine the **verbal, nonverbal, and cultural** elements relating to each co-culture, beginning with the Master Narrative and intercultural communication.

The *verbal* communication style of the WASP (white Anglo Saxon Protestants) best represents the verbal communication style of the dominant culture in the United States. Sixty-three percent of Americans speak English. Adopting the language of the early colonial settlers, English remains the most spoken language in the United States today, with this predominant language reaching 230 million.

Along with the verbal language shared by millions, the Master Narrative has unwritten linguistic patterns that are interesting to note. For example, the use of "small talk" is common with Americans. One may ask, "How are you?" and continue to walk away. This form of greeting, used daily, is confusing for those of various co-cultures who stop to answer the question. Thus, clichés and small talk

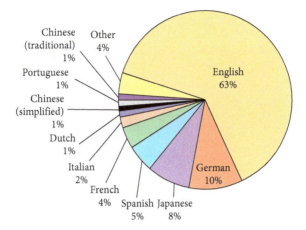

are just a few conventional communication patterns that can cause misunderstandings and dissonance.

Because **nonverbal communication** can influence as much as 93% of the communication process, it plays a key role in understanding one another. *Space, touch, time, smell, eye contact, body movement,* and *paralanguage* make up dimensions of nonverbal communication. Each dimension is used in different ways with different co-cultures; thus, problems emerge due to the ambiguous nature of nonverbal communication. This ambiguity, coupled with co-cultures that have different communication patterns, can result in misunderstandings in the interpersonal arena as well as in the workplace. For example, the indigenous people often use silence in interaction as a sign of dignity and respect, while the dominant culture views silence as a weakness, showing uncertainty.

Proxemics

Proxemics is humans' use of space. *Space* usage in the United States has been clearly established. In everyday conversation, personal space is preferred by the dominant culture (18 inches to 4 feet). Many co-cultures within the United States use intimate space, not personal space, for conversational distance. As the following chart reveals, the dominant culture likes large distances. This individualistic characteristic is no surprise, as the colonists and early settlers established themselves on large homesteads where land was vast.

Space Usage: Dominant Culture

Proxemics	Proxemics variations	Application
0" to 18"	Intimate	Touching; comforting
18" to 4'	Personal	Interpersonal interactions
4' to 12'	Social	Business setting; formal discussions
12' +	Public	Presentations; public affairs

Source. Adopted from Hall.

Haptics

Haptics is humans' use of touch. HAVE YOU HUGGED YOUR KID TODAY? This proclamation was a common phrase in the 1970s and represents the dominant culture's use of *touch (haptics)*. The United States is considered low contact and does not use intimate space (0 to 18 inches) for everyday conversation. Sharing touch is usually kept for private settings, and public displays of affection are frowned upon. Friends walking hand in hand, which is common around the world, is not a normal sight for Americans.

"Lost time is never found again."
Benjamin Franklin

Chronemics

The Master Narrative views *time (chronemics)* as monochronic in nature, adhering to strict schedules and viewing time as an important commodity: *Waste not, want not; time is money.* If one group does not use time in the fashion of immediacy, that group would be labeled "lazy" or "unmotivated." Many U.S. co-cultures follow more of a polychronic schedule, focusing on the relational aspect of the interaction while being flexible with promptness. As we will see in the upcoming chapters, this Master Narrative has a profound effect on those that do not fit this nonverbal philosophy.

Oculesics

The last nonverbal cue to be examined is the Master Narrative's use of *eye contact (oculesics)*. When interacting in any setting, direct eye contact is preferred for both males and females. This form of oculesics shows assertiveness and competence, two variables the dominant culture favors. Of course, direct eye contact with many of our nation's co-cultures may be considered rude and immodest.

The third circle in our examination is the **cultural** variable, consisting of a culture's *values and beliefs*. The Master Narrative provides the United States rituals and traditions that have become institutionalized throughout American society. For example, the early colonists established what we today call Thanksgiving. After arriving on the shores of Massachusetts and meeting the indigenous population, a gathering took place in 1621 where the indigenous people afforded the new visitors sustenance at a very crucial moment of their survival.

Survival struggles, such as starvation and disease, led the United States to become highly individualistic and independent. Hofstede's research on cultural variability and value systems places the U.S. dominant culture as the most individualistic country in the world. As seen on the following page, the United States is also categorized as masculine, which shows a strong male dominance in society. Statistics support this view, with only 4% of women holding CEO positions in Fortune 500 companies today and earning about 80 cents for every dollar earned by males. This power distance is much larger in co-cultures within the United States.

Individualism score: 91 (world average: 55)
Masculinity score: 62 (world average: 43)
Power distance score: 40 (world average: 64)
Uncertainty avoidance score: 46 (world average: 45)

Along with the values that constitute the Master Narrative, another cultural element to investigate is a concept called *worldview*, a group's perception of their beliefs, their deity, and how they see their existence. A worldview well established early on was accomplished with the importing of Christianity from England. Though the indigenous peoples had their own spiritual foundations, their worldview was unacceptable with the newly emerging Master Narrative. It was not long before the indigenous peoples were forced to take on this new religion, solidifying Christianity and continuing the goal of Manifest Destiny. As seen below, Protestantism remains the predominant religion today, with over half of Americans following this worldview.

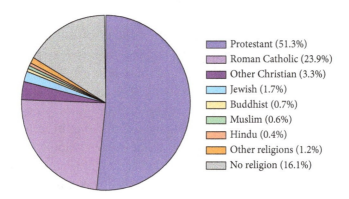

- Protestant (51.3%)
- Roman Catholic (23.9%)
- Other Christian (3.3%)
- Jewish (1.7%)
- Buddhist (0.7%)
- Muslim (0.6%)
- Hindu (0.4%)
- Other religions (1.2%)
- No religion (16.1%)

The establishment of the Master Narrative has developed over time into its present-day status, unquestioned and unexamined. The purpose of this text is to reverse this trend by questioning and examining this undisputed and universal American norm.

Historical Figures and Rhetorical Orations

"We are the nation of human progress, and who will, what can, set our limits to our onward march."
    John L. O'Sullivan (1813–1895)

"A little flattery will support a man through great fatigue."
    James Monroe (1758–1831)

"If men were angels, no government would be necessary."
    James Madison (1751–1836)

"No man will labor for himself who can make another labor for him."
    Thomas Jefferson (1743–1826)

Selected Bibliography

Adams, M. B. (Ed.). (2007). *Teaching for diversity and social justice* (2nd ed.). New York: Routledge.

Aguirre, J. A. (2010). *American ethnicity: The dynamics and consequences of discrimination* (7th ed.). New York: McGraw-Hill Education.

Brown, M. K. (2003). *Whitewashing race: The myth of a color-blind society* (1st ed.). Los Angeles: University of California Press.

Bush, M. E. (2011). *Everyday forms of Whiteness: Understanding race in a "post-racial" world* (2nd ed.). Lanham, MD: Rowan and Littlefield.

Elias, S., & Feagin, J. R. (2016). *Racial theories in social science: A systemic racism critique* (1st ed.). New York: Routledge.

Foner, E. (1998). *The story of American freedom* (1st ed.). New York: Norton.

Hall, E. T. (1959). *The silent language.* New York: Fawcett.

Hofstede, G. (2001). *Culture's consequences: Comparing values, behaviors, institutions, and organizations across nations.* Thousand Oaks, CA: Sage.

Oakes, J. E. (2017). *Of the people: A history of the united states with sources* (3rd ed.). New York: Oxford University Press.

Takaki, R. T. (2008). *A different mirror: A history of multicultural America* (rev. ed.). New York: Little, Brown.

US Census. (2014). "Language usage in the United States."

Zarya, V. (2016). "Female Fortune 500 CEOs are poised to break this record in 2017." *Fortune,* December 22. Retrieved from http://fortune.com/2016/12/22/female-fortune-500-ceos-2017

Credits

- Fig. 2.5: Source: https://commons.wikimedia.org/wiki/File:Cultivation_of_tobacco_at_Jamestown_1615.jpg.
- Fig. 2.6: Source: https://commons.wikimedia.org/wiki/File:JohnWinthrop.jpg.
- Fig. 2.7: Source: https://commons.wikimedia.org/wiki/File:General_George_Washington_at_Trenton_by_John_Trumbull.jpeg.
- Fig.2.9:Source:https://commons.wikimedia.org/wiki/File:Benjamin_Franklin_by_Joseph_Siffrein_Duplessis.jpg.
- Fig. 2.10: Source: https://commons.wikimedia.org/wiki/File:Religions_of_the_United_States.png.
- Fig.2.11:Source:https://commons.wikimedia.org/wiki/File:John_O%27Sullivan.jpg.
- Fig. 2.12: Source: https://commons.wikimedia.org/wiki/File:James_Monroe_02.jpg.
- Fig. 2.13: Source: https://commons.wikimedia.org/wiki/File:James_Madison.jpg.
- Fig. 2.14: Source: https://commons.wikimedia.org/wiki/File:Gilbert_Stuart_Thomas_Jefferson.jpg.

3 | The Collision of History and Intercultural Communication

"People fail to get along because they fear each other; they fear each other because they don't know each other; they don't know each other because they have not communicated with each other."

Dr. Martin Luther King Jr.

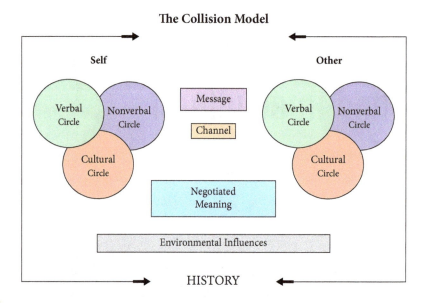

The Collision Model

The story of human interaction is an interdependent, continually changing process. The above Venn diagram demonstrates its interdependent nature. This model consists of several key components: verbal communication, nonverbal communication, and culture, couched in the historical context. *Self* and *other*, as well as the negotiation process, are also key components of the model. As we begin this examination, we hope to keep in mind that history influences the dynamics and nature of communication, and reciprocally, communication on history. Utilizing the Collision Model, a synergetic picture is provided as a tool for our journey of examining the record of human interaction.

The Components of the Collision Model

History: The *Lens* used as a frame to analyze the communication process

There are many perceptual lenses that can be utilized when analyzing interaction. In this text, we have chosen history and its rich insights to couch the analysis of each co-culture being examined. In light of the time frame to be used, starting from colonial America to present, the historical context that we'll be relating to is commonly known as the "American Experience."

Environmental Influences: The external and internal noise that is present in the communication process

Interpersonal interactions involve private and public noise that impedes the sharing of meaning. Psychological noise, such as our self-talk, is quite strong and is difficult to penetrate. Coupled with navigating the inner disturbances, we have physical noises that also challenge the communication process. These environmental noises, such as doors slamming or music playing loudly, affect the ability to listen clearly to the message being sent.

Self and Other: The participants in the interaction

The "self" is the sender and encoder of the message. The "other" receives the message and decodes it. This process is simultaneous, with the sender and receiver switching back and forth in their roles.

Message: The topic of conversation being shared

The message is the content and relational dimensions being transmitted. The "self," as the encoder, creates the topic and shares it with "other," the decoder, who is on the receiving end.

Channel: The medium in which you express the message

Historically, the channel has been a face-to-face experience or a simple written letter. In light of today's technological means of sending messages, the channel has changed dramatically. These new transmissions may include social media channels such as our use of the Internet, cell phones, and Facebook. The modalities change daily.

Verbal Circle: The written and spoken language of a group of people

Both written and spoken communication involve shared symbols that enable people to understand each other. Your culture provides you specific linguistic rules used every day in interaction.

Nonverbal Circle: The sharing of language other than linguistic means

Humans speak volumes using nonverbal communication. Dimensions include space, touch, time, smell, eye contact, body movement, and vocalics (tone, pitch, volume, and rate). These dimensions can make up 93% of the communication process.

Cultural Circle: The values, beliefs, and identities of a group of people

Cultural patterns are what we practice daily, such as worship, work ethic, and family connections. These variables are unique to each co-culture within the United States.

Negotiated Meaning: The arrival of understanding between self and other

The ultimate goal of communication is to reach understanding. Through your interaction, a new shared meaning emerges. Thus, the newborn authenticity of the message is formed.

A Newly Forged Tapestry

As previously mentioned, this combined approach of U.S. history and intercultural communication takes on a unique lens by examining numerous *co-cultures* and their specific themes within the early American context. Each examination will commence with the historic perspective of group experiences and struggles. Following their historic journey, we will see the role of communication and the patterns that emerged during these historic times. By examining the verbal, nonverbal, and cultural dimensions (Collision Model), a renewed perception will emerge. Forthcoming, a deeper exploration will be presented to guide you through the chapters ahead.

The Collision Model: A Deeper Exploration

The following theoretical perspectives will provide more detailed explanation of the components of the Collision Model, beginning with history and followed by intercultural communication.

Historical Schools of Thought

Whether looking at effective communication styles or ineffective communication interaction, history provides the master key to unlocking the dimensions. As we examine the verbal, nonverbal, and cultural elements of co-cultures within the United States, a historical foundation is necessary to understand the complexities of history and its link to communication.

The role of perspective dominates the presentation of U.S. history. Taking this into account, scholars have categorized historical writings into four distinct schools of perspective: the Progressive School, the Consensus School, the New Left School and the School of Social History. Before delineating the specific aspects of each of these schools, a point of emphasis must be made with regard to the dominant role played by context or historical background. Those who record history typically project their facts through their own personal perceptual lens and worldview. These schools of thought represent that diversity.

The Progressive School

The Progressive School was molded by its unique historical setting of the late 1800s and the early 1900s. The focus was on reform and the changing of society for the better. The rise of industrialization and urbanization had created a degrading effect on the morality and living conditions of many Americans. As a result, numerous laws were passed to upgrade the standard of living via Prohibition, child labor laws, and consumer protection legislation. The 1906 Meat Inspection Act, as a stark example, outlawed the selling of horse meat under the label of "America's Finest Beef." In addition, one particular book came forth,

"*An Economic Interpretation of the U.S. Constitution*" written by Charles A. Beard in 1913, arguing that this famous document was written by and for the rich at the expense of the poor. As a result, this era produced historians who looked at history simply as a matter of group conflict; the haves versus the have-nots; the business owner versus the consumer; the rich versus the poor.

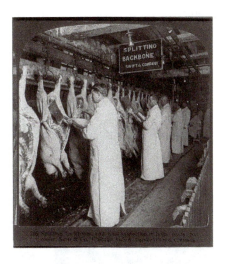

The 1906 Meat Inspection Act

Progressive School and Communication

In light of the Progressive School and communication, the forces that promoted the causes and needs of the "underdog" used particular communication styles which played a major role in this new era of reform. Such endorsed styles were evident, for instance, in the speeches of suffrage leaders who took on the male-dominated power differentials of the times. Rhetorical communication style manifested itself in Jeannette Rankin's speech to the House of Representatives after becoming its first female member in 1916.

"I may be the first woman member of Congress but I won't be the last."
Jeannette Rankin

Rankin, as the obvious underdog, employed a communication style that included the use of strong word choice that moved her constituents to action. Bearing that the women's suffrage amendment to the Constitution was not ratified until 1920, such public speaking by a woman at this specific time in U.S. history was wholly unacceptable to mainstream America. Included with Rankin were other strong orators for the underdog. Samuel Langhorne Clemens,

or Mark Twain, spoke in support of women's right to vote. Being a favored American author and public speaker, his humorous, thought-provoking communication style shed light on the movement.

In addition, Ida B. Wells, a public figure and powerful journalist in the 1890s, led the fight for the antilynching movement and established the first suffragist club for black women in 1913. As part-owner and lead editor of the *Free Speech* newspaper, she took routine opportunities to make her stance for social justice well known throughout the country.

"The way to right wrongs is to turn the light of truth upon them."
Ida B. Wells

The Consensus School

Because of the post-World War II paranoia known as the Cold War, *the Consensus School* emerged as the gatekeeper of the new status quo. This followed the chaos of the Great Depression and World War II, during which Americans were robbed of financial security and family continuity. The nationalism of the day presupposed that capitalism and democracy were the two keys of 20th-century civilization worldwide. This gave ground to a historical school that had the aim of producing security and continuity based on a citizenry that was loyal, faithful, and patriotic; the primary instrumentality to this end was K–12 public education. The American story became the story of the "good guy" who could do no wrong. As a prime example of this school's perspective, the romanticized portrayal of the arrival of

Christopher Columbus as a "discovery" reflects the mentality of this group of historians.

Consensus School and Communication

While the Progressive School utilized strong, action-oriented oratory, the philosophy of the Consensus School created an age of conformity in language behavior. These restrictions and limitations monitoring communication—from censored public information to the silencing and blacklisting of members of Hollywood—became the means in which this dominant view retained its power.

One way the government maintained this power was bypassing the Code of Wartime Practices for the American Press in 1942. Though it was not a mandatory restriction, many news outlets followed the code, in keeping with the loyal, patriotic citizen. Thus, as a government directive, reporters were required to accentuate the positive, as John Steinbeck depicted (right).

Communication was also disbursed in movie theaters, where masses could hear the message of the powerful. Most dominant was the radio, since most households had one in their possession. Daily interpersonal interactions with neighbors and friends kept the messages heard on the radio effective in shaping and reinforcing the Consensus School perceptions.

"There were no cowards in the American Army, and of all the brave men the private in the infantry was the bravest and noblest."
John Steinbeck

The New Left School

As widely accepted by many historians, this age of conformity sowed the seeds of rebellion that manifested in the 1960s. With this manifestation came a third historical school of thought, *the New Left School*. As a direct counteraction to the previous era of conformity, the 1960s posed a historical background of social upheavals and social revolutions, mainly consisting of the civil rights movement, the anti-Vietnam protests, the youth counterculture, and the rise of women's liberation. This perspective, as a result, portrayed American history as a story of hypocrisy, corruption, and self-aggrandizement. These historians view American history from a critical viewpoint, void of loyalty to maintaining the status quo. For example, the enlistment crisis during the Vietnam War (1954–1975) brought forth harsh opposition to government directives on the ground of social injustice, that is, the widespread casualties that were incurred among the poor, the young, and those of color.

The New Left School and Communication

"I love America more than any other country in the world and, exactly for this reason, I insist on the right to criticize her perpetually."
James Baldwin

From the side of communication, the historical context of the New Left School gave birth to a lexicon in American language, which created a chasm between the old and the young. A protest communication style, which voiced dissatisfaction with the status quo, was utilized in several arenas. The youth of the day expressed their protest-style communication in song, poetry, and public speaking. For example, James Baldwin, an influential author and activist, spoke on behalf of the struggles of this generation (left).

The unrelenting indignation toward the Vietnam War found its way in song and poetic expression. A strong visual image is represented in the lyrics of Billy Joel's "Goodnight Saigon."

We came in spastic like tameless horses
We left in plastic in numbered corpses...
And we would all go down together
We remember Charlie, remember baker
They left their childhood on every acre...
And we would all go down together.

Vietnam Memorial, Washington, D.C.

These momentous events in the history of the New Left School provided a forum for discontent, as we see in the rhetoric of the day. While this school of thought focused on a collective approach to change, our next school takes on a very individualistic perspective.

The School of Social History

The fourth and final school of thought has a unique environmental setting that coalesced into a particular perspective on history. With the demise of the political leadership of the 1960s, Americans in general began to lose hope in making major sweeping social changes. This gave rise to the designated "me" generation by the middle of the 1970s. A general consensus among Americans was to turn inward and seek personal satisfaction and material gain while casting a sneering contempt at government and social reform. Although pessimistic in nature, this historical context resulted in what is known as the *School of Social History*, wherein biographical information is used to trace the personal history of individuals. Unlike the other three previous schools of historical thought, here readers are permitted to reach their own conclusions by using individuals' stories as the foundation to interpret and extrapolate into a larger societal picture.

Historic Timeline: Four Schools of Thought

1893	Advancement of the "The Significance of the Frontier in American History" by Frederick Jackson Turner
1901	Vice president Theodore Roosevelt elevated to president as a result of McKinley's assassination
1906	*The Jungle* published by Upton Sinclair
1913	*An Economic Interpretation of the U.S. Constitution* by Charles A. Beard
1916	Jeannette Rankin becomes first female member of the House of Representatives
1919	Women's right to vote passed in Congress as the 19th Amendment
1920	Prohibition enacted nationwide with the 20th Amendment
1929	The Great Depression begins with the collapse of Wall Street
1932	Franklin D. Roosevelt elected the 32nd U.S. president
1941	The United States enters World War II with the Japanese attack on Pearl Harbor, Hawaii
1945	Japanese surrender (September) and the official end of World War II
1947	The rise of McCarthyism and the Second Red Scare
1953	Execution of the Rosenbergs for espionage on Behalf of the Soviet Union
1960	Election of John F. Kennedy as the 35th U.S. president
1964	Free speech movement at the University of California–Berkeley and passage of the monumental Civil Rights Act
1968	Dr. Nathan Hare establishes the first Black Studies Program at San Francisco State University
1973	Emergence of *Critical Race Theory* under the leadership of Richard Delgado and Jean Stefancic
1976	*Roots: The Saga of an American Family* published by Alex Haley

Within this perspective, the rise of Critical Race Theory (CRT) in 1973 provided a more defined and articulate approach to the role of the historical narrator. Though the School of Social History gave birth to the individual voice, CRT has switched the role of the narrative perspective to the co-cultures' storytelling, thus undercutting the presumptive legitimacy of the European "Master Narrative." (*Be sure to see the classic monograph entitled, "Critical Race Theory," by Stefancic and Delgado, published in 2001, for a fuller development of this monumental paradigm, portraying the history of co-culture resilience.*)

School of Social History and Communication

As seen in the School of Social History, intrapersonal communication lent itself to the individualistic approach to interaction. The storyteller is the encoder of the message. The sender emerges as the most important person in the interaction, and saving face becomes an important variable. (*Face* is our personal mask we show others daily in our communication interactions.) While the goal in the individualistic culture is to save our own face, other cultures, such as collectivists, tend to emphasize saving the face of the recipient. As referenced in the contextual background of the School of Social History, which rendered the "me" generation preeminent, face saving and concern for self became dominant.

"The only way for a woman, as for a man, to find herself as a person, is by creative work of her own."
Betty Freidan, founder National Organization for Women (NOW)

With this "me" emphasis came a second wave of feminism. Leaders such as Betty Freidan, Germaine Greer, and Gloria Steinem fought for individual rights for women. This emphasis resulted in a movement for development of personal empowerment.

Colloquial sayings representing the self became imbedded in the everyday lexicon during this time in history. "Believe in yourself" and "Live and let live" are a few with emphasis on the individual. Self-esteem building and a healthy self-concept became important personal goals, which in the past was considered unacceptable. The School of Social History provided the foundation for looking inward.

Shirley Chisholm, elected to Congress as the first black woman, sums up the School of Social History with this eloquent quote:

"We must reject not only the stereotypes that others hold of us, but also the stereotypes that we hold of ourselves."

Shirley Chisholm

Selected Bibliography

Delgado, R. A. (Ed.). (2000). *Critcal race theory: The cutting edge* (2nd ed.). Philadelphia: Temple University Press.

Feagin, J. R. (2012). *Racial and ethnic relations* (9th ed.). Upper Saddle River, NJ: Pearson Education.

Kitano, H. H. (1997). *Race relations* (5th ed.). Upper Saddle River, NJ: Prentice Hall.

Loewen, J. W. (2007). *Lies my teacher told me: Everything your American history textbook got wrong* (1st ed.). New York: Touchstone.

Oakes, J. E. (2017). *Of the people: A history of the United States with sources* (3rd ed.). New York: Oxford University Press.

Olson, J. S. (1994). *The ethnic dimension in American history* (2nd ed.). New York: St. Martin's Press.

Omi, M. A. (2015). *Racial formation in the United States* (3rd ed.). New York: Routledge.

Ting-Toomey, S., & Chung, L. C. (2004). *Understanding intercultural communication*. New York: Oxford University Press.

Credits

4 | The Indigenous Experience
The First Collision

"From where the sun now stands, I will fight no more forever."

Chief Joseph, 1877

History: A Lens of the Collision Model

Chief Seattle's Treaty Oration,1854

The Indian's night promises to be dark.
Not a single star of hope hovers above his horizon.
Sad-voiced winds moan in the distance.
Grim fate seems to be on the Red Man's trail
and wherever he will hear the approaching footsteps
of his fell destroyer and prepare stolidly to meet his doom,
as does the wounded doe that hears the approaching
footsteps of the hunter.

No greater example of failed human interaction and ensuing human suffering is laid before us than the plight of the original Americans. Though the history of the indigenous people can be estimated to go back thousands of years, the tip end of their present story (as in the last 400 years) is where we will begin our investigation of this co-culture and its interaction with the European invasion of the American continent.

The Threefold Devastation of the American Indian

The dimensions of devastation can be framed into three levels: physical, cultural, and social. These three variables emerged from the historical events of the destructive human interaction that took place between the first Americans and the much later arriving British. The demolition that took place physically, culturally, and socially represent the threefold devastation of America's first people.

Physical Devastation

In looking at the staggering statistics alone, the physical devastation is clearly one of moral exclusion (see the pyramid of failed communication, p. 13). From 1607, with the initial arrival of the British colonists, the first Americans confronted an onslaught that diminished their population over the next 300 years by 90%. Statistics show that the original population of the 500 tribal nations at the time of British intrusion was 2.5 million. By 1890 the estimated Indian population was down to 250,000 in the continental United States. The last major act of annihilation took place at Wounded Knee, South Dakota, in 1890 (see timeline, p. 56).

The Great Dying

While battles were numerous and even beyond documented records, the impact of disease was the major factor of casualties for the first Americans. The introduction by the Europeans of measles, smallpox, and even the flu transitioned into major epidemics among these populations. As a result, contagion took more lives than the military did. For example, the Arawak were decimated to sheer extinction within 50 years. Thus, the term the *Great Dying* was coined by the Indians as an expression of the universal suffering brought on by European diseases.

Cultural Devastation

The next dimension of devastation lies in the conflict of value systems that existed between the American Indian and the European colonist. Initially, the approach to the use of *land* set off an irreconcilable dichotomy. While the Indian viewed land as a gift of stewardship from Mother Earth, the European believed personal ownership and fencing was vital to individual wealth and prestige. As a result, any treaty was merely an expression of two different worlds miscommunicating, with the Indian being cheated and deprived methodically. At the same time, the reverence toward the natural environment expressed by the Indian was seen as superstitious and passive in the eyes of the capitalistic European.

While the American Indian was powerfully collective and *family* based, the British colonists brought in a wave of capitalistic focus on individualism and the self. With a successful tobacco enterprise, John Rolfe (1612) laid a foundation for the thrust of commercialism that would override the first Americans' group orientation and welfare. This created a divide that was insurmountable and never to be bridged. The Indian backbone of collective identity would be bombarded and continue to erode over the next centuries.

The devastating European influence on the American Indian land and family did not, however, diminish the spiritual core of this group.

Social Devastation

As a result of the European Americans' terms and conditions for the first Americans being that of "convert or be destroyed," the breadth and depth of exclusion can be seen in the ostracizing of America's indigenous population. Not only the overt expulsion of forced land removal but the ensuing concept of America's reservation policies point to a form of hostage taking never before seen in modern history. Events such as the Trail of Tears, along with the government's chasing down of the Nez Percé under Chief Joseph's leadership, point to the federal endorsement of Indian social annihilation, thus rendering them to the top of the pyramid of failed communication—morally excluded.

Boarding School

The wholesale stripping of the identity of indigenous people was embodied in the forced Americanization of the youth generation, in which boarding schools were employed to achieve these goals through routine and drastic detachment.

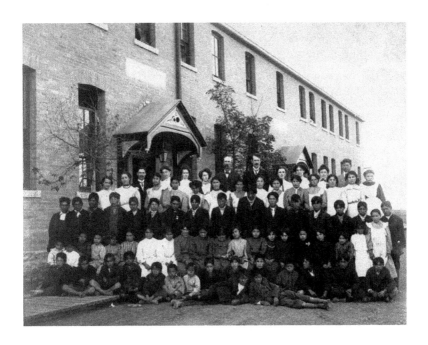

Not only were Indian youth stripped outwardly of their identity (hairstyle, attire, language, rituals, and traditions), their oppression was internalized. This self-hatred and internalized oppression resulted in the universal destruction of generations of youths. As a result, the native population was forced to abandon its historic and innate verbal, nonverbal, and cultural dimensions (see the Collision Model) for that of the dominant culture.

In light of the cultural blinders traditionally presented by the Consensus School regarding the American Indian, the School of Social History affords a biographical, lived-experience perspective as a true and myth-debunking representation of the first Americans. These two schools of thought will emerge when analyzing the indigenous communication styles.

Historic Timeline: Indigenous Peoples

1616	A smallpox epidemic decimates the indigenous population in New England
1621	One of the first treaties between British colonists (Plymouth Pilgrims) and indigenous people (the Wampanoag Tribe) enacts peace
1622	The Powhatan Wars commence between indigenous peoples and British colonists and continues for 12 years
1636	The Pequot War takes place in Connecticut and Rhode Island
1680	King Philip's War as a result of the resistance among the indigenous population in southern New England
1756	Enactment of the Scalp Act placing a bounty on the scalps of indigenous adults and children by Governor Robert Morris of Delaware
1772	Eighty percent of the Arikara people die of smallpox and measles over an 8-year period
1786	The Northwest Ordinance enacted to exercise "good faith" to honor the property, rights and liberty of the indigenous populations
1790	The first U.S. Census includes slave and free African Americans while excluding indigenous populations
1803	The Louisiana Purchase doubles the size of the United States at the hidden expense of indigenous populations
1804	Lewis and Clark "expeditions" into indigenous lands commissioned by President Thomas Jefferson
1814	Close of the Creek War as the single largest cession of territory in the Southeast with 14 million acres of Creek land lost
1833	Legislation passed making it unlawful for indigenous people to remain within the state of Florida
1838	The Trail of Tears forced removal
1868	Enactment of the Nez Percé Treaty as the last treaty between the U.S. government and indigenous people
1890	Massacre at Wounded Knee, South Dakota, ends in the slaughter of close to 300 Sioux people by the U.S. Army

The Verbal Circle: A Lens of the Collision Model

In examining the verbal communication styles of the indigenous people, it is acknowledged that the remarkable distinction within each tribe's individual richness could never be presented here. As a result, we will highlight the commonalities found in several tribal entities.

Verbal language of the indigenous people is one of indirect communication. The use of direct communication is considered disloyal and disrespectful to the "other" in interaction. The focus, therefore, is on the face saving of others. Most tribal communication patterns are considered *high context*. Chief Joseph, in the following quote, exhibits his wisdom when communicating with low-context leaders from the Master Narrative:

> *It does not require many words to speak the truth*
> *Good words do not last long until they amount to something...*
> *Good words will not give me back my children...*
> *Good words will not get my people a home where they can live in peace...*
> *I am tired of talk that comes to nothing. It makes my heart sick when I*
> *remember all the good words*
> *and all the broken promises.*

After looking at the historical events of our early peoples, the decrease in population affected the decrease in shared language. Before the arrival of the Europeans, there were 15 million speakers throughout the Western Hemisphere, and approximately 2,000 languages were used. The indigenous people, during this time, spoke 300 separate tongues among the 1.5 million natives. By the mid-20th century, after the European conquest, two thirds of the indigenous languages were gone. Today among the indigenous populations, only 1,000 persons per language utilize their native tongue, with most speaking English as well. This bilingual usage resulted from their tribal language coupled with English, the spoken language of the conquerors.

One exception to these above statistics is the Navajo. The Navajo speak Navajo, which is a subgroup of the Athabaskan language family.

It is the most commonly spoken tribal language in the United States, with over 150,000 individuals speaking this tongue. Sadly, the end result has been that many indigenous languages have become extinct. Scholars studying the oral languages of the current tribes have made an effort to record the language in its oral form and transcribe it to written form so as to preserve the oral tradition.

The Oral Tradition: Storytelling

As a distinctive trait among the indigenous people, storytelling is a major language variable to be explored. Storytelling, as the earliest form of communication, provides a common foundation for a shared identification and worldview of a particular group. Specifically, this co-culture passes down customs and tales of tribal life along with core beliefs regarding creation stories and the origins of humankind. These beliefs are expressed in music, dance, and poetry.

An example of oral tradition.

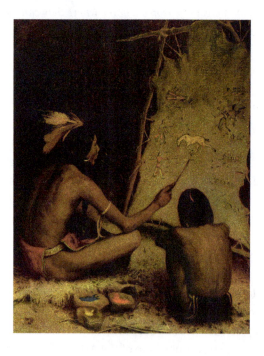

Silence

The beauty and diversity of the indigenous co-culture's communication style is grounded in its pairing of humanism and nature. This contemplative nature is conveyed in indigenous peoples' use of silence. Silence is a form of quietness and stillness within. This became a historic tool to navigate and survive the onslaught of aggressive invaders. If angry or uncomfortable, remaining silent was necessary. This modality of communication was interpreted by the dominant culture as a sign of passivity and nonparticipation, whereas from the indigenous standpoint, silence is a desired characteristic of an extraordinary person. Representing their peaceful and serene nature, their use of silence shows a deep respect for elders and their wisdom. On the contrary, an immediate response is a demonstration of immaturity by the sender of the message.

The Nonverbal Circle: A Lens of the Collision Model

Space

The use of space among the indigenous population is designed to increase a trusting environment. Sharing space provides a spiritual connection and increases the connectedness of the tribal members. We see this manifested in their early dwellings, with tribes creating their camps in a circular design. The desire to share space with family members is present today. With over 300 reservations in the United States, tribal members continue to live in collective settings. As a capstone to European colonization with its genocidal form of moral exclusion, the indigenous people were indeed stripped of their land but not of their dignity and collective resilience.

Touch

Members of the dominant culture in the United States are considered low-contact communicators, while the indigenous peoples' use of touch plays a different role. Their orientation toward touch is to

provide healing powers and signs of affection toward the in-group. Babies are often swaddled as a means of unbroken reassurance. Light touch is appropriate when greeting people, with hugging between family members preferred. As a point of contrast, the dominant culture believes that a stern handshake conveys confidence. As a result, the lightly touched handshake is often misinterpreted as a sign of passivity by the Master Narrative.

Eyes and Face

With over 25,000 facial action codes, (FAC's) the human face and eyes send complex messages. From the way we use our eyebrows to the way we frown can be documented and interpreted by experts. But for the everyday communicator, these nuances are barriers to understanding the message sent. For the indigenous population, use of direct eye contact (which is the predominant style of the dominant culture) is considered disrespectful and irreverent. Throughout the history of "negotiations" with the European colonizers, the indigenous leaders' use of indirect eye contact was misinterpreted as a sign of deception worthy of suspicion.

Time

Time is a cyclical dimension for the indigenous peoples. Based on sunrise and sunset, the indigenous people connect to nature. This perception is evident in their use of time today. Most tribes are considered polychronic, which views time in a fluid fashion. Being "late" is often considered on time for this group. Terms such as "reservation time" and "Eskimo time" represent this concept. Many experts consider the indigenous people as present oriented, which is a focus on immediacy. Placed in the context of their precarious history, this orientation became a tool of navigation and survival. Totem poles,

as seen right, provide an example of a rich background in ancestral roots, family identity, and social hierarchy. This tendency of the indigenous people toward past orientation is profound.

Gestures

The *high-context* communication style of the indigenous people reveals itself in the use of gestures. Gestures are unique in each tribe and usually are directly linked to the values and beliefs of the specific group. With a plethora of languages used by tribal groups, the Plains indians, for instance, created a sign language that was shared by multiple tribes. The illustrations below convey their innovative approach to bridging the language barriers.

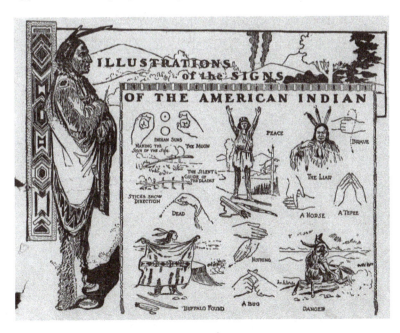

The Cultural Circle: A Lens of the Collision Model

"One Does Not Sell The Land People Walk On."
Crazy Horse

Beliefs and Values

The cultural circle examines the beliefs and values of a group of people. The indigenous people place strong roots in the spiritual dimension, with all aspects of life being connected holistically. Each tribe has its own myths and legends, which are passed down with their oral traditions. With the forced infusion of Christianity into this co-culture, we now see a curious blend of both worldviews within some of the tribes. Today we see their spiritual strength and richness expressed in individual and collective settings.

Kluckhohn and Strodtbeck's research on value orientations concluded that each cultural entity has its own unique view on nature. Nature, for the indigenous people, is central and foundational to their worldview. Their goal is to live in harmony with nature and use only what is necessary for survival. As Chief Joseph stated:

"The earth is our mother. She should not be disturbed by hoe or plough. We want only to subsist on what she freely gives us."

Cultural Orientations

Another aspect of their belief system is their view on family. The indigenous people possess strong *collective* roots, very different from the Master Narrative's highly individualistic perspective. With most tribes living in community, whether on the reservation or within the dominant culture, the extended family is pervasive. They would also be categorized as *masculine,* with the male figure as the decision maker and the females in supporting roles. Though there are matriarchal tribes, most are patriarchal in nature, with a higher *power distance* present. Elders are viewed with great wisdom and respect and thereby highly esteemed throughout the group membership.

The strong identity of the indigenous people is represented in their traditions and rituals, such as pow wows (below). Pow wow, meaning "spiritual leader," is a gathering held by many tribes within the United States. Artifacts, spiritual dances, and native foods are on display to celebrate their ancestral roots. Handmade headdress feathers are proudly worn, as the feathers represent a commitment to all things living.

Key Figures and Rhetorical Orations

"Let us put our minds together and see what life we can make for our children."
Chief Sitting Bull, 1831–1890

"When I think of my past life, and the bitter trials I have endured, I can scarcely believe I live, and yet I do; and, with the help of Him who notes the sparrow's fall, I mean to fight for my down-trodden race while life lasts."
Sarah Winnemucca, 1844–1891

"We are vanishing from the earth, yet I cannot think we are useless or else Usen would not have created us. He created all tribes of men and certainly had a righteous purpose in creating each."
Geronimo, 1829–1909

"Let our last sleep be in the graves of our native land."
Chief Osceola Seminole, 1804–1838

Selected Bibliography

Colbert, D. (Ed.). (1997). *Eyewitness to America: 500 years of America in the words of those who saw it happen* (1st ed.). New York: Random House.

Feagin, J. R. (2012). *Racial and ethnic relations* (9th ed.). Upper Saddle River, NJ: Pearson Education.

Healey, J. F. (2015). *Race, ethnicity, gender, & class: The sociology of group conflict and change* (1st ed.). Los Angeles: Sage.

Kluckhohn, F.R., & Strodtbeck, F.L. (1960). *Variations in Value Orientations*. New York: Row and Peterson.

Olson, J. S. (1994). *The ethnic dimension in American history* (2nd ed.). New York: St. Martin's Press.

Omi, M. A. (2015). *Racial formation in the United States* (3rd ed.). New York: Routledge.

Sen, S., & Wizner, A. D. (2016). *Communications strategies for a diverse world* (3rd ed.). Dubuque, IA: Kendall Hunt.

Takaki, R. T. (2008). *A different mirror: A history of multicultural America* (rev. ed.). New York: Little, Brown.

Ting-Toomey, S., & Chung, L. C. (2004). *Understanding intercultural communication*. New York: Oxford University Press.

Zinn, H. (2015). *A people's history of the United States* (2nd ed.). New York: Harper Perennial Modern Classics.

Credits

- Fig. 4.7: Source: https://commons.wikimedia.org/wiki/File:Plains_Indian_ Sign_Language_-_dec_28_1900.jpg
- Fig. 4.8: Source: https://pixabay.com/en/crazy-horse-usa-mountains-moun-tain-2646548/.
- Fig. 4.9: Source: https://commons.wikimedia.org/wiki/File:2007_National_ Pow_Wow_Grass_Dancers.jpg.
- Fig. 4.10: Source: https://commons.wikimedia.org/wiki/File:Chief_Sitting_ Bull.jpg.
- Fig. 4.11: Source: https://commons.wikimedia.org/wiki/File:Sarah_Winnemuc-ca_Hopkins.jpg.
- Fig. 4.12: Source: https://commons.wikimedia.org/wiki/File:Osceola.jpg.
- Fig. 4.13: Source: https://commons.wikimedia.org/wiki/File:Geronimo,_as_ US_prisoner.jpg.

5 | The African American Experience

Collision and Race

*"One ever feels his twoness — an American, a Negro;
two souls, two thoughts, two unreconciled strivings;
two warring ideals in one dark body, whose strength
alone keeps it from being torn asunder."*
W. E. B. Du Bois

History

The story of the Africans transplanted from their homeland by coercion is one of two horrendous outcomes: the demolition of individual identity and the destruction of the collective strength that constituted the core of the Africans. As a result, the two foremost and basic dilemmas on behalf of African Americans would be the pursuit of individual dignity and the safeguard of collective rights. This striking avenue of American history portrays a glaring example of failed human interaction, full of ethnocentrism and rising to a level of moral exclusion (see the "Pyramid of Failed Communication," p. 13).

U.S. Slavery: The African Holocaust in North America

The first 20 souls from Africa arrived at Jamestown, Virginia, in 1619. Aboard a Dutch vessel headed to enslavement in the Caribbean, these 20 individuals were intercepted and brought to the Virginia colony not as slaves but as indentured servants. However, by 1640 in the colonies of Virginia and Maryland, the institution of indentured servitude was amplified to lifetime bondage for those of African ancestry. This untimely conversion resulted in 225 years of an institution where humans were treated as nonentities and considered highly expendable; thus, they were morally excluded.

The Nature of American Slavery

While the devastating characteristics of this institution on the humanity of those of African ancestry were manifold, we will examine a few of the major aspects that emerged as lasting and significant. First of all, the forced extraction from the homeland and the destruction of the family unit decimated the Afrocentric identity and core of existence. In addition, the stripping of ancestral names barricaded the African into a corner of nonentity. Take the overt and outward mistreatment that the American slave endured; this dimension of internal oppression is largely whitewashed by the Consensus School of history, only to be later revived by the New Left School of history's research findings and documentation.

With the first characteristic of slavery being the annihilation of the identity of the African American, another definitive characteristic is the dehumanization process in the plantation life from day to day.

This process involved the complete stripping of any human dignity or sense of personal value. The Africans were treated as chattel in the sense that they could be sold away from each other at any time, they were not allowed to venture into literacy of any kind, and the female was sexually violated on a universal scale. Hurled upon these disgraces were the endless epithets and derogatory titles to encapsulate their less-than-human and inferior status. The mortality rate and infant mortality rate betrays the complete disregard of human life as a result of unfettered racism. Many dimensions of resistance were employed by the enslaved African American, such as slave revolts, poisonings of the master class, and both individual and collective runaways. Both the famous slave revolt led by Nat Turner in 1831 and the Underground Railroad escape mechanism led by individuals such as Harriett Tubman point to the extreme tools of survival under such oppression.

Navigating through centuries of slavery reveals the third characteristic of American slavery to be noted. Both the individual and collective notions of inner strength and resilience came from a slave

"I was the conductor of the Underground Railroad for eight years, and I can say what most conductors can't say; I never ran my train off the track and I never lost a passenger."

Harriett Tubman

culture that flourished over the lifetime of this institution. The main vehicles for this phenomenon were those of spiritual foundations, family connections, and modes of encrypted communication that gave life and lasting impact to this community under ruthless oppression. Although a large body of research from the scholars of the New Left School and the School of Social History have brought these characteristics forth in the past four decades, the Consensus School maintained the dominant culture's narrative that has dominated public education and social discourse.

American Apartheid: Jim Crow Segregation (1619–1964)

Whether slave, indentured servant, or free man, the African American continued to suffer a sustained form of oppression. One of the most ironic and paradoxical aspect of American history has been this record of racial distinctions that resulted in a systemic inequality. This is the era known as American segregation.

Segregation Formed (1619–1861) and Segregation Challenged (1861–1877)

The systematic approach determined by skin color alone first took place with the arrival of the first 20 Africans in 1619. Although unofficial, there was an unspoken quarantine placed on this group of individuals merely because of their genetic characteristics (as revealed in the 1620 census, in which they were not acknowledged by individual names). As the decades progressed and colonial America evolved into a republic, racial segregation became a documented practice within the U.S. Constitution and following legislative acts.

In the early 1820s segregation was embodied in a lasting symbol known as the *Jim Crow* character, devised by the Irish entrepreneur

T. D. Rice. Employed in America's first national pastime, the minstrels, African Americans were now symbolized as mindless buffoons, useful only for comic relief (played by white males in black makeup). This lasting stigma and myth of inferiority have left its footprints on the chronicles of American history to the present day. It was not challenged until the close of the Civil War and the advent of Reconstruction, America's first civil rights movement. But as history tells us, by 1877 the government's efforts toward racial equality were shot down by the keepers of white supremacy of the former South.

The caricature of Jim Crow.

Segregation Sanctioned (1877–1920) and Segregation Institutionalized (1920–1954)

Racial terror reigned throughout the South as a result of the close of Reconstruction and the withdrawel of Union troops. Linching and the Ku Klux Klan became the two primary gatekeepers of black subjugation. In 1896 the *Plessy v. Ferguson* decision reinforced the practice of racial segregation with its conclusive statement of "separate but equal." Not until the 1954 *Brown v. Board of Education* decision did the federal government intervene to put a crack in the foundation of racial separation, at least on paper with regard to public schools.

African American Leadership and Alternatives

The leadership alternatives taken by African Americans exist within three basic modalities:

*Coexistance and tolerance
*Defiance and withdrawal
*Expose and provoke change

In looking at the pre–World War II black response, there were several leaders who stood out in light of these three modalities. Booker T. Washington (1856–1915) exemplified the methodology of *coexistence and tolerance* by means of accommodating segregation in not seeking its immediate overthrow. David Walker (1796–1830) stood up for *defiance and withdrawal* by means of endorsing black militancy as the primary means to confront the evils of racial segregation. Lastly, Frederick Douglass (1818–1895) dynamically employed the methodology of *expose and provoke change* by demanding the application of constitutional rights to the black struggle for racial equality and integration.

W. E. B. Du Bois has played a significant role joining the late 1800s with the early 1900s in regard to impact in leadership. As the foremost sociologist and historian of black America, Du Bois's articulation of the inner dilemma of African Americans (labeled the double consciousness) defined the experience of those of African ancestry in its totality. As a cofounder of the largest and oldest civil rights organization in American history, Du Bois did indeed pass the torch to the post–World War II major leaders of the black struggle: Malcolm X and Dr. Martin Luther King Jr.

As James H. Cone has outlined in his masterpiece, *Martin and Malcolm and America* (2012), King and Malcolm X calibrated the African American struggle down to two sides of the same coin. King was the master of the struggle for collective rights. Malcolm, on the other hand, came forth as the master of self-identity and self-determination. As a result of these two landmark ideologies, the social landscape of American with regard to its black constituents was changed forevermore in

Historic Timeline: African Americans

1619	First 20 Africans are brought to Virginia as indentured servants
1640	John Punch becomes the first legally documented slave in the British colonies (Virginia)
1662	Virginia law passed subjecting children to their mothers' social status as slaves for generational continuation
1712	The New York revolt initiated by 23 enslaved Africans kill 9 whites
1770	Crispus Attucks killed in the Boston Massacre as the first American martyred patriot
1780	Pennsylvania becomes the first U.S. state to abolish slavery
1787	The Three-Fifths Compromise at the Constitutional Conventions relegates individuals of African descent to three fifths of a person
1794	Eli Whitney is granted a patent on the cotton gin
1816	The "Father of the Black Church," Richard Allen, establishes the African Methodist Episcopal Church
1820	The Missouri Compromise draws the geographical line of demarcation between the North (free states) and the South (slave states)
1829	David Walker, the "Father of Black Militancy," publishes his famous abolitionist pamphlet, "Walker's Appeal"
1831	The Nat Turner slave rebellion takes place
1839	Following the slave revolt aboard the *Amistad*, the U.S. Supreme Court grants freedom and the right to return to Africa to the kidnapped Africans
1849	Harriet Tubman escapes from slavery to Philadelphia to later become a coleader of the Underground Railroad
1857	The *Dred Scott v. Sanford* Supreme Court decision removes all geographical restrictions on slavery nationwide
1865	The 13th Amendment is passed as the first legal action to outlaw slavery
1872	P. B. S. Pinchback is sworn in as the first black member of the U.S. House of Representatives
1877	The Compromise of 1877 brings in the official collapse of Reconstruction
1881	Booker T. Washington opens the Tuskegee Normal and Industrial Institute in Alabama
1892	Ida B. Wells publishes *Southern Horrors: Lynch Law in All Its Phases*
1896	*Plessy v. Ferguson* Supreme Court decision makes "separate but equal" the law of the land

just two decades. The unique and distinctive efficacy of the communication styles of these two leaders is shown in root form as we explore the following evolution of African American language patterns.

The Verbal Circle

Africans arrived on the North American continent in 1619, bringing a myriad of native tongues from their homeland. These languages were forged with the European American English to create a unique style of communicating. With strong inflection and intense verbal communication style, African Americans are largely categorized as *low-context communicators*. This use of language benefited the African American during the era of American slavery.

To date, current language patterns of the African American include Ebonics, or the African American Vernacular English. This socially controversial verbal style does have its roots in strong language requirements. In spite of meeting basic language rules, such as syntax consistency, members of mainstream America have rejected its legitimacy. Legislative action was put in place to bar any future emergence of Ebonics in general public education.

As a result of ethnocentrism, African Americans have employed the skill of adaptation in communication, commonly known as code switching. *Code switching* is the ability to analyze one's audience and adapt to that particular setting. This communication strategy is utilized by the African American in everyday interaction. From the boardroom to the classroom, code switching is a survival tool and an instrument for daily identity management.

Oral Tradition

African Americans have a strong oral tradition, dating back to the first generation of slaves in North America. As a result of a strong emphasis and belief in the power of the word, a rich verbal language emerged. These exuberant language patterns were evident throughout the institution of American slavery and have been sustained up to the present day. Negro spirituals were shared in the picking fields of pain and oppression, as we see below in the song "Go Down Moses:"

Go Down Moses

African American Spiritual

When Is-rael was in E gypt's land, Let my peo ple go, Op pressed so hard they could not stand, Let my peo ple go. Go down, Mo ses, 'Way down in

bethsnotes.com

E- gypt's land,. Tell ol' Pha roah, to let my peo ple go.

These strong oral traditions continue to this day. The instrumental "I Have a Dream" speech (referenced below) by Martin Luther King Jr. includes many of the same patterns we see in the above song. His use of strong, clear repetition and rhythm coupled with storytelling and vivid, sharp pictures instilled a searing vision indelible through the generations:

"I have a dream that my four little children will one day live in a nation where they will not be judged by the color of their skin but by the content of their character"
Martin Luther King, Jr., August 28, 1963

The Nonverbal Circle

Space and Touch

The African Americans' use of space is infused with their use of touch. This co-culture is considered high contact, with close space enjoyed during communication. The use of intimate space (0" to 18") for personal interaction is preferred. This sharply clashes with the dominant culture's use of personal space (18" to 4'). Researches have observed a stark contrast between African American males and their white counterparts, with black males using more touch between themselves. In addition, black females touch twice as often as their white counterparts.

Eye Contact

Emmitt Till

Eye contact becomes another component in intimacy for this co-culture. African Americans prefer direct eye contact, especially when communicating with fellow blacks. Because direct eye contact has connotations of aggressiveness when used by this group in interracial interaction, careful consideration is taken when using this nonverbal cue. As seen in the era of slavery, direct eye contact was considered not only rebellious but unlawful. During the 100 years of racial segregation that followed the end of slavery, cases such as the lynching of Emmitt Till in 1955 point to the violation of direct eye contact and its consequences.

Time

The use of time among African Americans originates from their historic origins. Slavery lent itself to long hours, and time became invisible for the slaves, creating a polychronic environment. This polychronic approach remains today. Black people time (BPT), with its fluidity, goes against the dominant culture's use of a strong monochronic system. There are exceptions, such as within professional settings, when a more stringent adherence to time is expected. But the relational, collective African American enjoys the polychronic system.

The Cultural Circle

Beliefs and Values

The African American co-culture has a spiritual belief system originating over 400 years ago. Their strong commitment to Christianity emerged during the period of slavery in which they adopted the faith of the master class. With toil and sorrow, they turned to a spiritual development that sustained them with endurance and strength, blending their African spirituality. This commitment is apparent in the strong faith practiced today. Eighty-seven percent of African Americans are religiously affiliated, with 45% following the Baptist wing of Christianity.

Cultural Orientations

Hofstede's research on collectivism reminds us that many cultures live in community and not in a nuclear fashion. African American families historically are *collective.* The oppression of both slavery and segregation dictated the need for collectivism for the sake of navigating and survival. Eventually, however, they created a co-culture that flourished within itself. This collectivity remains today within the walls of their churches. But within the home, we find a strong *feminine,* matriarchal system, with 44% of females heading their households, while the majority within African American culture still holds to a *masculine* worldview. Standing outside of the norms of the dominant culture, African Americans find themselves in an ocean of individualism contrary to their cultural roots.

Collectivism and the African American family.

Power distance (the measure of how power is distributed) is clearly defined when examining African Americans. They would be categorized as a recipient of a very large power distance. The discrepancy between those in institutional power and most African Americans is stark. Within the system, there are inherent roadblocks to success for this co-culture, resulting in African Americans finding themselves at the low rung of the economic ladder. As reported by the U.S. Census Bureau in 2016, African Americans' net worth was significantly less than white families—a trend that has been historically without change.

Historic Figures and Rhetorical Orations

"Truth is powerful and it prevails."
Sojourner Truth, 1797–1883

"I got my start by giving myself a start."
Madam C. J. Walker, 1867–1919

"Fear of something is at the root of hate for others, and hate within will eventually destroy the hater."
George Washington Carver, 1860–1943

"Power concedes nothing without a demand. It never did and it never will."
Frederick Douglass, 1818–1895

Selected Bibliography

Hall, E. T. (1959). *The silent language*. New York: Fawcett.

Healey, J. F. (2015). *Race, ethnicity, gender, & class: The sociology of group conflict and change* (1st ed.). Los Angeles: Sage.

Hine, D. C. (2014). *African Americans, combined volume: A concise history* (5th ed.). Upper Saddle River, NJ: Pearson Education.

Hofstede, G. (2001). *Culture's consequences: Comparing values, behaviors, institutions, and organizations across nations*. Thousand Oaks, CA: Sage.

McCoy, R. (2011). "African American elders, cultural traditions, and the family reunion." *Generations* (blog), November 18. Retrieved from http://www.asaging.org/blog/african-american-elders-cultural-traditions-and-family-reunion

Olson, J. S. (1994). *The ethnic dimension in American history* (2nd ed.). New York: St. Martin's Press.

Omi, M. A. (2015). *Racial formation in the United States* (3rd ed.). New York: Routledge.

Roediger, D. R. (2008). How race survived U.S. history: From settlement and slavery to the Obama phenomenon (1st ed.). Brooklyn: Verso.

Scott, W. R. (2000). Upon these shores: Themes in the African-American experience, 1600 to the present (1st ed.). New York: Routledge.

Takaki, R. T. (2008). *A different mirror: A history of multicultural America* (rev. ed.). New York: Little, Brown.

Thompson-Miller, R. F. (2015). *Jim Crow's legacy: The lasting impact of segregtion* (1st ed.). New York: Rowman and Littlefield.

Zinn, H. (2015). *A people's history of the United States* (2nd ed.). New York: Harper Perennial Modern Classics.

Credits

- Fig. 5.4: Source: https://commons.wikimedia.org/wiki/File:Thomas-D-Rice-1832.jpg.
- Fig. 5.5: Paul Robeson, "Go Down Moses," http://www.bethsnotesplus.com. php56-15.dfw3-2.websitetestlink.com/wp-content/uploads/2014/07/Go-Down-Moses.png.
- Fig. 5.6: Source: https://commons.wikimedia.org/wiki/File:Martin_Luther_King_-_March_on_Washington.jpg.
- Fig. 5.7: Copyright © Image Editor (CC BY 2.0) at https://commons.wikimedia. org/wiki/File:14EmmettTillBefore_(2534273093).jpg.
- Fig. 5.8: Source: https://commons.wikimedia.org/wiki/File:Portrait_Category,_Gospel_Singer_160226-A-AJ780-020.jpg.
- Fig. 5.9: Copyright © 2011 Depositphotos/Monkeybusiness.
- Fig. 5.10: Source: https://commons.wikimedia.org/wiki/File:Sojourner_truth_c1870.jpg.
- Fig. 5.11: Source: https://commons.wikimedia.org/wiki/File:Madam_CJ_Walker _face_circa_1914.jpg.
- Fig. 5.12: Source: https://commons.wikimedia.org/wiki/File:George_Washington _Carver_c1910_-_Restoration.jpg.
- Fig. 5.13: Source: https://commons.wikimedia.org/wiki/File:Frederick_Douglass _c1860s.jpg.

6 | The Classless Caucasian Experience

Collision and the Trans-Atlantic Immigration

John Fitzgerald Kennedy, 35th president of the United States
(the only Irish American Catholic elected to office).

History

The American Consequence of European Immigration

The experience of immigration and exploitation for a large number of Europeans stands out as a glaring paradox in terms of "America, the land of the free." In these cases, repeatedly and categorically, the notion of white skin as distinctive and superior and thereby worthy of social privilege escapes the ideology within the Master Narrative mind-set. What spurred on this new wave of dominance over their fellow continental, European "brother" was a rise in the first quarter of the American 19th century of "nativism." The greater irony within the application of such a term was that now even the true native status of the indigenous peoples had not only been robbed and stripped away but "re-allocated" to the white European of the "highest stock"—American-born and WASP. This now became the identifiable class of privilege and power, much to the exclusion of those of European descent who were "otherwise."

A second powerful impulse that created the atmosphere of sanctioned discrimination against the classless European immigrant was the spike in "xenophobia" that arose simultaneously with nativism's widespread influence. The fear of outsiders—the definition of xenophobia at its base form—was a major force of thrust for the Master Narrative's wholesale discounting of the powerless European immigrants who brought over their unpalatable "motherland culture" and invasive religion so contrary to the true Protestant core beliefs.

Accompanying both nativism and xenophobia, as the third and final force of imposition was that commonly known as "nationalism"—which had risen to new heights with the close of the War of 1812 just three years later. America was now not only the "land of the free" but also the "only land free of savagery"—counting in the whole of Europe as well. So any group of European immigrants that didn't fit this threefold filter was bound to face endless waves of discrimination and ostracizing from those who either knowingly or unknowingly sided with the Master Narrative's ubiquitous application of normalization throughout early American society. "These people" were not "normal" and therefore were worthy of wholesale second- or third-class citizenship.

The Major Influx of the Classless Caucasian

As the 19th century approached its midway, the numbers of these "undesirables" increased at an alarming rate. The number of new European arrivals in the 1830s rose to 600,000, followed by 1.7 million more in the 1840s. In the 1860s the flow of European immigration was close to 2.5 million, constituting a capsizing on-slaught in the eyes of the status quo at that time. Coming primarily from the British Isles (especially southern Ireland) as well as Germa-ny, these newcomers experienced a mixed blessing of a sort: jobs and public schooling combined with public scorn and disdain.

The general American public was offended at this bulge of "for-eigners" according to a sixfold "observation" held universally and without question: (a) their sheer numbers were overwhelming and unacceptable; (b) they did not appear to be "desirable" citizens who could fit in; (c) they consistently broke the law and drank too much; (d) they were clannish and held to "their own" for no good reason; (e) they refused to accept the customs and practices of their newly adopted country; and (f) above all, they were poor and uneducated. Confusing causes with consequences, many white Americans held members of this population responsible for their own squalid living conditions, ill health, and burdensome presence that proved to be so odious to the majority of citizens.

An Example: The Irish Distinction

This is especially true for the Irish, who would account for one third of all immigrants to America from 1820 to 1860. They faced an economic downward spiral for several decades brought on by the demise of their basic staple, the potato, as well as the rampant exploitation and oppression of their anti-Catholic master class landowners, who effectively held the landless to a form of genera-tional slavery. With the infamous Potato Famine of 1845, Ireland's population dropped from 8 million to 6 million alone that year.

One million died from starvation and disease, while another 1 million set off for the United States in hope of a better future for their offspring. What they encountered, however, was anything but the anticipated "land of promise" of their dreams and aspirations. Not only were their common surnames quickly despised and repudiated, but also their sheer appearance, dress, and accent were objects of scorn and derision. Stereotyped as typically drunk, uneducated, and mindless, the Irish soon became the primary target of xenophobia, nativism, and nationalism in their worst forms.

During the 1850s immigrants from Ireland were blatantly ridiculed and caricatured as beast, subhuman, and of the lowest form of human-like entities, paralleled only by African Americans. Signs and newspaper advertisements that voiced this vitriol were rampant and unquestioned throughout the nation (especially on the East Coast), with the common refrain of "No Irish Need Apply." As a result, not only did imposed poverty and ghetto residential settings become their slice of the "American pie," their Catholic faith took on a new form of religious intolerance never witnessed before on such a level of intensity. The pervading WASP mentality of mainstream Americans found ample evidence of Irish religious allegiance to clerical bodies of the Catholic Church on a daily and weekly basis that fanned into flame an ever-growing level of antagonism, ridicule, and even violence from neighborhood to neighborhood. Vigilante groups arose to locally address this newfound "alien menace," such as the Sons of '76, the Sons of America, the Druids, and the Order of United Americans. Immigrants from Poland and Germany were often targets of these groups' other forms of social outcasting based on their surnames and accents as well.

As the Irish settled in the major cities of the Northeast, their desired pathway toward assimilation came forth in a gradual yet steady manner. Canal building and the railroad business eventually became forums to demonstrate a respectable work ethic and level of fortitude. Eventually, access to the local police force and local political office gave way to a more humane form of acceptance, primarily as a result of new and more odious wave of eastern and southern European immigrant hit the shores of the East Coast in the late 1800s and early 1900s due to the eruption of U.S. industrialization and urbanization.

The Xenophobic Trend: The Turn of the 20th Century

Now, especially with the Italians, the focus of nativism and nationalism found their expression of intolerance on a new 20th-century arena of the Master Narrative. At the height of this xenophobic eruption, the 1927 trial and execution of Sacco and Vanzetti provided a big window into the mind-set and atmosphere of these turbulent times, at least as far as European immigrants were concerned. The U.S. federal government even entered the fray of wholesale discrimination by passing the restrictive 1921 Immigration Act and the 1924 Origins Act, diminishing the growing population base of the "European undesirables" that were flooding the nation at the turn of the 20th century.

Historic Timeline: The Classless Caucasian

1740	The start of a decade where Irish make up 90% of indentured servitude in a some colonies due to the devastation of the Irish Potato Famine
1790	The Anti-Catholic Penal Laws removed in England, allowing emigration to America
1816	Another revival of natural calamities in Ireland resulting in widespread famine and poverty
1845	The initiation of the five-year Irish potato famine provoking major Irish emigration to America
1850	Irish account for nearly one half of all immigrants to America
1855	The anti-Catholic Know Nothing Party surfaces with a platform to limit or end the influence of Catholic Irish Americans
1877	The Long Strike of 1875 enacted by the Irish Molly Maguires, who protested discrimination and working conditions
1891	Opening of Ellis Island in New York Harbor by a congressional act empowered to inspect and deport "undesirable immigrants"
1921	The Emergency Quota Act passed to restrict the number of immigrants to America
1924	Further immigration restrictions via the Immigration Act passed by Congress
1927	Sacco and Vanzetti executed by the U.S. government as a result of nationwide xenophobia

The Verbal Circle

The United States today includes over 34 million Irish Americans, who account for the second largest co-culture. Historically, the Irish spoke Gaelic, a Celtic language commonly spoken in Ireland and the Scottish Highlands. England's influence added another language to their repertoire, English. Today little of the Gaelic tongue is present.

The Irish Americans brought with them a strong oral tradition. Because of the lack of written Gaelic, the Irish relied on the verbal transmission of their culture. The influence is marked in the United States today. With riddles, poems, and storytelling, the Irish immigrant has added much to the spoken word.

High- and Low-Context Communicators

Because of the harsh treatment historically, the Irish Americans were discouraged to share their verbal roots. They were forced to be *high context,* which conflicted with their natural oral traditions. Presently, the use of strong verbal skills coupled with the ability to code switch when necessary has made the Irish American *low-context* communicators as well. Assimilating with the Master Narrative linguistically has provided the Irish American acceptance among the dominant culture.

With the Irish American enjoying verbal competence, the written word has been added to their repertoire. One strong example of this ability is seen in the works of the famous author F. Scott Fitzgerald (right). His writings have enjoyed a generational influence with the people of the United States.

"Show me a hero and I'll write you a tragedy."
F. Scott Fitzgerald

The Nonverbal Circle

Space and Touch

The Irish Americans like their personal space (chart, p. 28). In interactions, 18" to 4' is a comfortable distance interpersonally and in the workplace. They are a low-contact culture, touching less than most co-cultures in the United States. The Irish American, in this category, is similar to the dominat culture's use of these nonverbal cues.

Time

Edward T. Hall describes the polychronic perspective as one that is elastic. Time cannot be stagnant but is a flexible variable. The Irish American holds this approach to chronemics. Family and relationships are paramount; thus, following a rigid timeline is challenging. This may be considered rude and inconsiderate; thus, it is important for those in superior positions to be aware of this nonverbal dimension.

Eye Contact

Direct eye contact is considered appropriate in the United States. Historically, due to extreme discrimination against Irish Americans, eye contact was not encouraged when interacting with the dominant culture. Submissive behavior was appropriate, since "Irish Need Not Apply." Today Irish Americans' use of eye contact is similar to that of the Master Narrative. Direct eye contact in the workplace is common for this co-culture.

Kinesics

Hall's categorization of kinesics is highlighted in the Irish Americans' use of traditional clothing. Most noticeable are the annual St. Patrick's Day celebrations throughout the United States on March 17. This day, rooted in Irish history, recognizes the death of St. Patrick, the patron saint of Ireland. Green items are familiar in these events, such as leprechauns and shamrocks. The leprechaun, mischevious bearded men, are depicted by many. The shamrock represents the Christian Trinity. Both are symbols deeply rooted in the Irish American bedrock.

Cultural Circle

BELIEFS AND VALUES

Irish Americans are traditionally religious. The Irish immigrants, arriving with the early settlers, kept their Protestant foundation and established this form of Christianity in the colonies. Later arrivals were predominantly Roman Catholic. The same mix is present today. The domant religion of the Irish American is Protestantism, followed by Catholicism. The historic lack of influence among the

Master Narrative has produced only one Irish Catholic president, John Fitzgerald Kennedy.

A representation of Irish American Christian faith can be found in the shamrock; the good luck charm of the Irish.

The Shamrock: The Father, Son, and Holy Spirit

Cultural Orientations: A Lens of the Collision Model

The extended family plays a dominant role for Irish Americans and thus is *collective* in nature. Kinship was historically important and remains so within this group today. For example, this co-culture encourages marriage within the Irish heritage, strengthening their identity and genealogical lines. Divorce rate, partially due to this foundation, is lower than most co-cultures within the United States. This past-oriented group celebrates its strong roots in religious rituals and celebrations. From St. Patrick Day parades to corned beef and cabbage, this co-culture has affected the Master Narrative in a profound way.

Women historically have played strong matriarchial roles in the family. Their ability to keep the family together during challenging times was influential to future generations. With the man as the head of the household, he was clearly the decision maker and bread winner. Today, as with the dominat culture, Irish Americans are considered *masculine.* Though the roles may not be as stark as they were, this co-culture remains male oriented.

The *power distance* between the dominant culture and the early Irish immigrant was large. As history tells us, they were replaceable and nonentities (moral exclusion). Though eight Irish Americans signed the Declaration of Independence (below) in 1776, it would take more than a century for this group to gain respect and acceptance within the dominant culture.

Historical Figures and Rhetorical Orations

"A scandelous old Irishwoman" unjustly executed during Salem Witch Trial, Ann Glover (d. 1688).

"Lost in a land where many didn't want them, violent, without skills, the Irish were in need of rescue. This was Hughes's flock."

Archbishop John Hughes, 1797–1864

"Our words — our lives — our pains — nothing! The taking of our lives — lives of a good shoemaker and a poor fish-peddler — all! That last moment belongs to us — that agony is our triumph."

Nicola Sacco (1891–1927) and Bartolomeo Vanzetti (1888–1927).

Selected Biography

Colbert, D. (Ed.). (1997). *Eyewitness to America: 500 years of America in the words of those who saw it happen* (1st ed.). New York: Random House.

Davidson, J. W. (2009). *U.S.: A narrative history* (1st ed., Vol. 2). New York: McGraw-Hill.

Feagin, J. R. (2012). *Racial and ethnic relations* (9th ed.). Upper Saddle River, NJ: Pearson Education.

Hall, E. T. (1966). *The hidden dimension.* New York: Doubleday.

Healey, J. F. (2015). *Race, ethnicity, gender, & class: The sociology of group conflict and change* (1st ed.). Los Angeles: Sage.

Hofstede, G. (2001). *Culture's consequences: Comparing values, behaviors, institutions, and organizations across nations.* Thousand Oaks, CA: Sage.

Olson, J. S. (1994). *The ethnic dimension in American History* (2nd ed.). New York: St. Martin's Press.

Omi, M. A. (2015). *Racial formation in the United States* (3rd ed.). New York: Routledge.

Roediger, D. R. (2008). *How race survived U.S. history: From settlement and slavery to the Obama phenomenon* (1st ed.). Brooklyn: Verso.

Takaki, R. T. (2008). *A different mirror: A history of multicultural America* (rev. ed.). New York: Little, Brown.

US Census. (2014). "Irish Americans." Retrieved from http://evolve.elsevier.com/Giger.

Zinn, H. (2015). *A people's history of the United States* (2nd ed.). New York: Harper Perennial Modern Classics.

Credits

7 | The Mexican American Experience

Collision and Borders

"It is better to die on your feet than to live on your knees."
Emiliano Zapata (1879–1919)

As an iconic figure during the Mexican Revolution (1910) and an enduring symbol of Mexican nationalism, Emiliano Zapata stood armed and in proud defiance of the powers of oppression. The Mexican American, throughout historic events, utilized this same defiance in the face of injustice and destruction.

As we explore the Latino/a population, the focus will be on the Mexican American. With 33 million Mexican Americans in the United States, they stand as the predominant co-culture, representing 65% of the Latino/a population. The influence of Mexican Americans in the United States is commanding, and they constitute the fastest growing co-culture in America today.

History

The Mexican Americans

Whether Spanish or British European military exploitation, the indigenous people of Mexico and the eventual Mexican Americans have a story of resilience in spite of tragic land takeover. As we consider the demolition of the Aztec empire, the Consensus School of history initiates its Master Narrative portraying the indigenous people as weakened victims alone. The formation of the Mexican in the northernmost part of this nation-state would encounter the British American riding on a wave of Manifest Destiny with its consequence of unimaginable destruction and confiscation.

The Theft of Northern Mexico: The Lone Star Republic

As the westward takeover proceeded into the southwestern region, the American pretension was to assimilate into the region we call today the state of Texas. The agreed-upon terms for settlement according to the Mexican government's wishes included no slavery, adoption of the Catholic faith, and no permanent land ownership. Used as a means to buttress the indefensible northernmost region against Comanche raids, this policy opened the door to American greed and land grabbing. Having started in 1821, the Texas

Revolt, as it is called by consensus authors, initiated a rebellion against Mexican government control. With the bloodshed finalized in 1836, the 9-year existence of the Texas republic had commenced, with its legacy as the Lone Star Republic. By 1845, just prior to the U.S.–Mexican War, Texas was officially annexed into the United States.

The Mexican–American War of 1846–1848

Driven by the call of Manifest Destiny, the U.S. military instigated a military conflict with the Mexican people. The disputed clash at the Rio Grande afforded a door for American exploitation by claiming "American blood has been shed on American soil." With this ominous catch phrase, President Polk was able to declare war on Mexico with the full consent of the U.S. Congress. The following 18 months of bloodshed and lopsided military dominance culminated in the Treaty of Guadalupe Hidalgo. The United States paid $15 million to the Mexican government for physical damages yet walked away with northern Mexico in its hands. As a result, this confiscated region transferred over to the following states of the U.S. republic: California, Arizona, New Mexico, Colorado, Utah, and Nevada. To add insult to injury, the 1851 Congressional Land Act reduced the Mexican people in this region to landless, second-class people. The passage of this new legislation required U.S.-recognized proof of land ownership, thus stripping the former landowners of all their property.

The Glaring Paradox: Foreigners in Their Own Land

Over the next 100 years, a series of dehumanization and discrimination would dominate the tale of America's newest "alien." Numerous

A zoot suit.

key events promoted this newfound "alien" label, such as the 1920 Border Rush (to answer the call for cheap labor in the United States); the 1943 Zoot Suit Riots in Los Angeles (bloodshed instigated by soldiers on furlough upon Latino night life); the institution of the Bracero Program of 1942–1965 (a seasonal entry-work program based on short-term contract workers); and Operation Wetback of 1950–1954, which deported over 1 million persons of Mexican descent, though oftentimes unconstitutionally.

The Chicano Movement and Civil Rights

The grassroots struggle for civil rights for people of Mexican ancestry took on the label of the "Chicano" movement under the leadership of the likes of Cesare Chavez in the 1960s. Focusing on the unionization of migrant farmworkers, this mobilization eventually became successful in overcoming the exploitation of the discriminatory large companies that dominated California's agricultural empire. The popular United Farm Workers became a powerful tool for change by provoking even American consumers to participate in boycotts of various produce available in stores. By 1970 Jose Angel Gutierrez founded the Latino Political Party and a strong-arm action group known as La Raza Unida. Resistance to entrenched discrimination, now underway on numerous fronts including higher education and Latino/a scholars, carried over into the new millennium over such issues as English-only debates, border and immigrant legal clashes, and nationwide economic challenges.

"There has to be someone willing to do it."
Cesare Chavez, 1964

Historic Timeline: The Mexican Americans

1691	Texas is made a separate Spanish province
1718	The highly influential mission at San Antonio is founded
1776	The founding of San Francisco is celebrated by the Spanish
1821	After declaring independence, Mexico allows for the first European Americans to settle in the Mexican state of Texas
1829	Slavey is abolished by the Mexican government
1835	Euro-Texans and Tejanos unite to resist and rebel against the repressive government of Mexico
1845	After 9 years of independence, the Lone Star Republic of Texas is annexed to the United States
1846	U.S.–Mexican War begins over territorial disputes
1862	The Homestead Act is passed, thereby stripping Mexicans of vast land in the West
1902	U.S. Congress passes the Reclamation Act, which further "legally" strips land from those of Latino descent
1917	The Immigration Act passed by Congress enforces a literacy requirement on all immigrants
1925	The U.S. Border Patrol is created by the U.S. government
1932	Initiation of Mexican deportation close to half a million by the U.S. government before 1940
1943	The Zoot Suit Riots in Los Angeles
1951	The Bracero Program is enacted by the U.S. government, opening the border to Mexicans as seasonal agricultural workers
1954	Operation Wetback deports 4 million individuals of Mexican descent under federal legislation

The Verbal Circle

The verbal style of Mexican Americans is warm and inviting. In the arena of family and familiarity, there is a comfortable exchange in their native tongue, Spanish, creating a climate for open interaction. Combined with the ability to use effective interpersonal skills at home, they also use direct, dignified language when required. As an example of this language pattern, the 1960s lent itself to this rhetoric. With boycotts brought on by the migrant worker leadership due to intolerable working conditions and exploitation, activists employed their skills. This is well represented by this quote from Dolores Huerta, cofounder of the United Farm Workers of America:

"Don't be a marshmallow. Walk the street with us into history. Get off the sidewalk. Stop being vegetables. Work for justice. Viva the boycott!"
Dolores Huerta

Most Mexican Americans speak both English and Spanish. In the Mexican American home, one third are bilingual (using both Spanish and English), while the other two thirds use either one or the other. This strongly bilingual group has a population of 55 million and is our largest co-culture. Thus, it is no surprise that Spanish plays a significant role in American society today. This is most evident in the southern border states. Interestingly, the trait of being bilingual is more prominent in urban settings and among laborers.

The Mexican American employs patterns from the *low- and high-context communicator*. With verbal characteristics of the low-context communicator, this group uses gestures and nonverbal nuances that make it high context as well. This stands in contrast to the dominant culture's task-oriented, direct communication style.

The Nonverbal Circle

Space and Touch

Abrazo! This Spanish word for "embrace" encapsulates the style of the Mexican Americans. Their use of touch is a common nonverbal characteristic. Their demonstrative behavior is used to affirm one another, which assists in building a strong identity. Because of their use of touch while communicating, they employ intimate space for personal interactions; 0" to 18" is a comfortable distance for Mexican Americans to converse. This co-culture, with its value on modesty, manifests a certain level of restraint in its patterns of public touch.

Eye Contact

Prolonged eye contact is considered rude among Mexican Americans. Directness can be disrespectful. This indirect use of eye contact aligns with the importance of modesty and care for others in interaction. One popular folktale teaches us that the evil eye, or *mal ojo*, when cast toward an infant, can result in a curse. Only through the use of touch with the infant is the curse removed.

Time

Historically, the siesta—literally, the "sixth hour"—was a traditional midday resting period for many Mexican Americans. This Mexican tradition is still practiced in the United States in some barrios, or neighborhoods. The term *mañana* (tomorrow) emerged from this chronemic lens. This polychronic nature is adjusted in the workplace when essential. Though the monochronic Master Narrative is practiced by Mexican Americans, the concern for relationships and family still supersedes a task orientation.

Culture Circle

Beliefs and Values

Mexican Americans are homogenous when it comes to their faith. They are overwhelmingly Christian, with over 60% following the Roman Catholic religion and almost 20% identifying themselves as Protestants. Founded by Franciscan priests in 1573, the first Catholic missions established these historic religious roots. This belief in Catholicism brought rituals and traditions that are practiced to this day. Celebrations such as Day of the Dead and celebrating Our Lady of Guadalupe are cultural norms in many barrios. The picture of the Lady of Guadalupe is commonly seen in Mexican American businesses, on public display.

Our Lady of Guadalupe.

La Familia

La familia, or "the family," is an important cultural element for Mexican Americans. With many living in extended family settings, this *collective* co-culture depends on the family for support and loyalty. The *abuela*, or grandmother, provides a traditional foundation for Mexican American families. It is common to see family names that include the maternal and paternal side, showing respect for both mother and father. The role of the male, though, is the dominant force in the family and is the decision maker. Thus, the *machismo* or *macho* image of the Mexican American male remains. This masculine orientation is seen in the need for both control and saving face in interpersonal interactions.

This male-dominated leadership lends itself to a *high power distance* within the home and in the workplace. A large power distance is also present in the picking fields of America, where migrant workers, predominantly of Mexican descent, are an invisible population. More than 3 million seasonal farmworkers assist the U.S. agricultural community, earning as little as $10,000 per year, drastically below the poverty level in the United States. The Master Narrative allows this power distance to meet the needs of the dominant culture.

Historical Figures and Rhetorical Orations

"We are free, truly free, when we don't need to rent our arms to anybody in order to be able to lift a piece of bread to our mouths."
Ricardo Flores Magon, 1874–1922

"My painting carries with it the message of pain."
Frida Kahlo, 1907–1954

"Action must be taken at once; there is no time to be lost; we shall yet see the oppressors' yoke broken and the fragments scattered on the ground."
Miguel Hidalgo, 1753–1811

"My sole ambition is to rid Mexico of the class that has oppressed her and given the people a chance to know what real liberty means. And if I could bring that about today by giving up my life, I would do it gladly."
Pancho Villa, 1878–1923

Selected Biography

Colbert, D. (Ed.). (1997). *Eyewitness to America: 500 years of America in the words of those who saw it happen* (1st ed.). New York: Random House.

Condon, J. (1985). *Good neighbors: Communicating with the Mexicans.* Yarmouth, ME: Intercultural Press.

Desmond, M. A. (2016). *Race in America* (1st ed.). New York: Norton.

Feagin, J. R. (2012). *Racial and ethnic relations* (9th ed.). Upper Saddle River, NJ: Pearson Education.

Gangotena, M. (2004). "The rhetoric of la familia among Mexican Americans." In A. González, M. Houston, & V. Chen (Eds.), *Our voices: Essays in culture, ethnicity, and communication.* (pp. 93–103). Los Angeles: Roxbury.

Hall, E. T. (1966). *The hidden dimension.* New York: Doubleday.

Healey, J. F. (2015). *Race, ethnicity, gender, & class: The sociology of group conflict and change* (1st ed.). Los Angeles: Sage.

Olson, J. S. (1994). *The ethnic dimension in American History* (2nd ed.). New York: St. Martin's Press.

Omi, M. A. (2015). *Racial formation in the United States* (3rd ed.). New York: Routledge.

Takaki, R. T. (2008). *A different mirror: A history of multicultural America* (rev. ed.). New York: Little, Brown.

US Census. (2014). "Mexican American language usage."

Zinn, H. (2015). *A people's history of the United States* (2nd ed.). New York: Harper Perennial Modern Classics.

Credits

8 | The Chinese American Experience

Collision and Crossing the Pacific

Economic Desperation and Exploit

The initial wave of immigration from China was initiated by the 1849 Gold Rush in California. The grim realization of the Chinese miner, as portrayed in the photo above, points to the plight created by the all-too-familiar union of economic desperation and economic exploitation. In spite of such a troublesome start followed by congressional acts of exclusion, this co-culture eventually laid the foundation of a promising story for Asian Americans.

According to today's social setting, Asian Americans find themselves in the forefront of success among co-cultures. Conveniently labeled the "model immigrant," this group has excelled in the areas of income growth and education. Surprisingly, Asian Americans have surpassed Hispanics as the fastest growing racial group in the United States.

Chinese: 4,010,114
Filipino: 3,416,840
Indian: 3,183,063
Vietnamese: 1,737,433
Korean: 1,706,822
Japanese: 1,304,286

The above population chart ranks Chinese Americans first among Asian immigrants. Because of their strong presence in the United States, the chapter's emphasis will be placed on this group. In addition, a snapshot of other Asian Americans will be provided.

History

The Chinese Americans

Immigration of Asians to the United States began mainly in the middle of the 19th century. For the very same reasons the Europeans came, the Chinese also arrived: years of famine, poverty, and unemployment in their homeland. The initial aspirations of the Chinese were to come to this country, work, and send the funds back home. The majority of the Chinese who came were poor, male villagers who were forced to leave their wives and children. By 1851, 25,000 Chinese were working in California due to the Gold Rush. By 1888, 25% of the railroad workers employed by the Central Pacific Railroad were Chinese. Because of the willingness to quietly work, they filled the labor force vacuum that was then in the forefront. With a lot of work to do and shortage of workers, the Chinese were actually welcomed initially, yet clearly separated from their white counterparts in the workplace and at home. As the economic conditions continued to worsen in the United States, the discrimination against the Chinese greatly increased. The degree of antagonism progressed from quiet separation to outright discrimination and violence, finalized with legislative action and congressional acts.

For example, in 1862 the U.S. Congress passed a law forbidding American ships to transport Chinese immigrants to America. Twenty years later, because of fear and ignorance, Congress passed the *Chinese Exclusion Act of 1882*, subject to future renewal. This was the first piece of legislation in U.S. history to ban a specific racial group from entering the United States. In 1910 the Angel Island Inspection Station was built in San Francisco to enforce this law.

Anti-Chinese Violence

Physical hostility escalated in the 1880s against the Chinese immigrants. Communities throughout the West Coast as well as Nevada, Wyoming, and South Dakota were subjected to racial intimidation as well as physical attacks. For example, a wave of anti-Chinese riots and incidents took place in the state of Washington. Seattle's China town was burned down in 1885, and 2 months later, 300 Chinese

Americans were expelled from Tacoma. With moral exclusion rampant throughout the West, this co-culture was considered expendable to the point of resulting in the passage of the *Scott Act of 1888,* which permanently banned Chinese immigration to the United States. Not until almost 60 years later, in 1943, was this blatant rejection of Chinese lifted for immigration renewal.

Gary Locke, Governor of Washington (1997–2005).

Chinese Americans today, in spite of this disgraceful history of mistreatment, have emerged as a self-determined co-culture, constituting a strong thread in the American tapestry. Besides having a strong presence in higher education and entrepreneurial successes, they have made small but distinctive strides in the political arena, such as Gary Locke, the first Chinese American governor in the United States.

The other group of Asian immigrants that represented a significant number of new arrivals were those of *Japanese* descent. They too, as with Chinese Americans, experienced exploitation and discrimination within the American labor force structure. Arriving in the late 1800s in the Pacific Northwest, they found employment in the railroad industry in accompaniment with racial discrimination. Race riots surfaced in the 1920s and resulted in wholesale evacuation of Japanese Americans from various towns throughout the Northwest. This crystalized in the following years to outright banning of their owning or leasing land. With the advent of World War II in 1941, the discrimination reached the level of moral exclusion, as embodied in Executive Order 9066, which ordered the removal of 120,000 Japanese Americans from the West Coast to 10 inland concentration camps located in isolated areas within seven states. Over 66% of those interned were constitutionally protected American citizens. The Japanese Americans lost their homes, jobs, businesses, and savings as a result of this federal act of internment. This mass incarceration represented one of the most serious violations of civil liberties in all of American history. Although released in disgrace and depravity with the close of World War II in 1945, the Japanese American was not granted naturalized citizenship until 1952, with the passage of the Walter–McCarran Act.

Historic Timeline: Chinese Americans

1844	China and the United States sign treaty for "peace, amity, and commerce"
1848	Gold is discovered in Northern California, initiating the Gold Rush and boom and bust of the mining industry
1850	Chinese American population in United States reaches 4,000, primarily in the West
1860	Chinese American population jumps to 35,000 (out of 31 million nationwide)
1865	Chinese laborers are recruited to work on the Transcontinental Railroad by the Central Pacific Railroad
1871	Anti-Chinese and Anti-Chinese American violence breaks out in Los Angeles and spreads to other cities
1882	The U.S. government passes the Chinese Exclusion Act
1941	China becomes a newfound ally as a result of the Japanese attack on Pearl Harbor
1943	Congress reverses exclusionary stance: all exclusion laws dropped and Chinese granted path to citizenship
1950	Chinese American population reaches 150,00 out of national total of 150 million

The Verbal Circle

Verbal characteristics of Asian Americans are consistent with their historic experiences and confrontation with various forms of xenophobia.

Chinese Americans

Statistics reveal there are over 2.8 million Chinese American speakers in the United States, and the Chinese language is the third most *spoken* language in America. Specifically, the Chinese Americans' verbal language consists of many dialects; for example, Cantonese and Mandarin. The Cantonese dialect is typically used in Chinatowns, while people coming from China or Taiwan tend to use the Mandarin. In addition, the English language is taught early, resulting in Chinese Americans being multilingual speakers. The *written* language consists of unlimited characters and is not considered an alphabet. This creative form of communicating is illustrated below.

地球 水 元素
earth · water · element

火 空氣 動力
fire · air · power

血漿 和平 太陽
plasma · peace · sun

Asian Americans, in summary, speak English (63%), coupled with their native tongue. When speaking Chinese, emphasis on tonation reveals the meanings in the message. Because of a vast array of vocalics, the Chinese American language cannot be generalized. Japanese Americans have a strong English pattern with their use of Japanese as well. Filipinos, on the other hand, speak Tagalog more often than English. East Indian Asians have in their repertoire English and Hindi. It is evident that the Asian Americans, with their rich diversity in language patterns, add much to the tapestry of languages spoken in America.

High-Context Communicators

Losing face is a not desired among Chinese Americans when communicating. This Mandarin phrase, translated into *humiliation,* is a part of their culture and history. Because of the need to save face and to dismiss this humiliation factor, the speaker's image conveyed to others is both vital and essential. Revealing a harmonious, inclusive face when interacting with others is the goal. Speaking loudly is a sign of disrespect and a loss of self-control. The use of silence is valued. With emphasis on indirect verbal interaction, they are process-oriented. As the dominant U.S. culture is goal oriented, this can become a barrier in communication interactions. Chinese Americans tend to be receiver centered, with the need to satisfy the request of the interactant, to the extent that the word "no" is not common in their vocabulary. Understanding the implicit and non-verbal nuances of the high-context Chinese American increases the opportunity for mutual, satisfying interactions.

NO! IS NOT IN THE VOCABULARY!

The Nonverbal Circle

Space and Touch

The Chinese American culture is a low-contact co-culture. During interaction, touching is not a constant. Public displays of affection are frowned upon. Same-sex interactions with friends lends itself to increased touch, which is acceptable. You may observe Chinese Americans, as well as many Asian American groups, walking side by side, and with best friends, arms linked together. Intimate distance is acceptable under these terms, but personal distance is needed when speaking face-to-face.

Eye Contact

The use of indirect eye contact is favored by Chinese Americans. Respect for the individual in interaction is revealed in their use of this nonverbal cue. Direct eye contact is viewed as impolite and inappropriate, especially when speaking with someone of higher status. Thus, while talking with Chinese Americans, one may feel they are not interested in the conversation due to the lack of direct eye contact. On the contrary, their emphasis on the "other" in interaction is consistent with the theme of honor and reverence.

Kinesics

Kinesics, body movement, is an insightful dimension in E. T. Hall's nonverbal cues. For example, the use of *bowing* is prevalent among co-cultures from eastern Asia. It is used as a greeting but also as a sign of respect for one in a position of relevance. A full bow reveals the power distinction in the dyad. A slight bow shows more of an equal status. Today common greetings from Chinese Americans include a slight bow or the Western handshake.

Clothing is another component of kinesics and one that Chinese Americans embrace. Though Western clothing is predominant, Chinese Americans celebrate special occasions with traditional attire. Some brides wear the customary wedding color, red, for their gown, showing their anticipation of a happy life. This corresponds to the variance of the dominant culture, where white is the symbol of an optimistic future.

Time

An inch of time is an inch of gold.

Chinese Americans' history contributed to their perceptions of time. Slavery and moral exclusion were experiences that shaped a strong monochronic lens. The use of time in a scheduled, systematic way was wise and prudent for the Chinese American. *Time is more valuable than money,* and completion of a task is the paramount goal today. However, the Chinese American couples this approach with polychronic tendencies. Relationships, status, and respect in the interaction take precedence and may slow the process. As a result, if additional time must be given to a task, it is acceptable and desired. With Chinese Americans living in a dominant culture that views time with similar values to their own, the monochronic approach is not uncomfortable.

In addition, the traditional Chinese calendar, called the luni–solar calendar, is worth exploration. In contrast to the solar calendar used in U.S. culture, the Chinese calendar is based on the completed phases of both the moon and the sun. As seen on the following page, the

Chinese calendar is a familiar sight in the United States. Displayed in many places of business as well as homes, it is a cultural norm in American society. The calendar substantiates important dates, such as the Chinese New Year. The signs of the zodiac are symbolized in animal forms, as seen below.

The Cultural Circle

Beliefs and Values

Over 50% of Chinese Americans do not consider themselves affiliated with any particular religion or worldview. The predominant worldview in America for this group is Protestantism (22%), followed by Buddhism (15%). Chinese traditions and rituals are still practiced in the United States, especially the Chinese New Year. With Chinese American being the largest Asian ethnicity, it is celebrated with great vigor across the nation. *Good luck* and *family harmony* are some of the goals of this holiday. Children, for example, are given *good luck money* to stave off evil spirits. Golden dragons can be seen in parades, and favorite foods, such as pig and duck, are prepared with historic emphasis.

Cultural Orientations

The Chinese American comes from strong patrilineal roots that are embedded in the Chinese culture. This cultural emphasis of *masculinity,* in which the male plays a dominant role, has continued in the United States. In many cases in America today, the male still remains responsible for care of the elder members of the family, with the female role a significant force of support. Living in one dwelling with relatives is not uncommon, with multigenerational settings very popular in the United States. If not living under the same roof,

you may find family members living in close proximitry, reinforcing the *collective,* family-oriented nature of Chinese Americans.

Harmony again emerges as the core motivation for this co-culture's communication pattern. The *yin yang* (adjacent) represents the union of female–male energies, bringing together both a balance and harmony in life.

Thus, whether it be in the home or the workplace, the elements of harmony and loyalty are paramount for Chinese Americans. This ability to save the face of others and not "rock the boat" is a strong example of the Consensus School communication patterns, staying within the boundaries of the dominant culture's acceptable behavior.

> *"Dharma is not upheld by talking about it. Dharma is upheld by living in harmony with it."*
> Gautama Buddha

Historical Figures and Rhetorical Oration

Survived forced migration from China to oppresive Idaho mining camps.
Lalu Nathoy, aka Polly Bemis (1853–1933)

Prominent Chinese community leader who resisted the anti-Chinese agitation in Hawaii.
Goo Kim Fui, 1835–1908

"As residents of the United States, we claim a common manhood with all other nationalities, and believe we should have that manhood recognized according to the principles of common humanity and American freedom."

Chinese-American horticulturalist, known as the "Citrus Wizard."
Lue Gim Gong, 1870–1925

Wong Chin Foo, 1847–1898

Selected Bibliography

Davidson, J. W. (2009). *U.S.: A narrative history* (1st ed., Vol. 2). New York: McGraw-Hill.

Feagin, J. R. (2012). *Racial and ethnic relations* (9th ed.). Upper Saddle River, NJ: Pearson Education.

Healey, J. F. (2015). Race, ethnicity, gender, & class: The sociology of group conflict and change (1st ed.). Los Angeles: Sage.

Kim, Y. Y. (2003). "Intercultural personhood: An integration of Eastern and Western perspectives." In L.A. Samovar & R.E. Porter (Eds.), *Intercultural communication: A reader* (10th ed.). Belmont, CA: Wadsworth/ Thomson Learning.

Kitano, H. H. (1997). *Race relations* (5th ed.). Upper Saddle River, NJ: Prentice Hall.

Olson, J. S. (1994). *The ethnic dimension in American history* (2nd ed.). New York: St. Martin's Press.

Omi, M. A. (2015). *Racial formation in the United States* (3rd ed.). New York: Routledge.

Takaki, R. T. (2008). *A different mirror: A history of multicultural America* (rev. ed.). New York: Little, Brown.

Ting-Toomey, S., & Chung, L. C. (2004). *Understanding intercultural communication*. New York: Oxford University Press.

US Asian-American population. (2011). "What Defines Asian Americans?" Pew Research Center.

Zinn, H. (2015). *A people's history of the United States* (2nd ed.). New York: Harper Perennial Modern Classics.

Credits

9 | Keys to Unlocking the Master Narrative
The Collision Model Illuminated

The 1964 Civil Rights Act emerged as a line of demarcation between promises pronounced and promises delivered (at least on paper).

As we have briefly examined the journeys of various ethnic groups over the span of early and mid-American history, the reoccurring theme of the role, impact, and influence of the Master Narrative has been a core funnel experientially for each group, regardless of their widespread variation and starting points. As mentioned in the opening chapter, the Master Narrative can be defined as a mechanism of exploitation by the means of assumed originality and legitimacy when it comes to the unfolding of the "American story." It normalizes one unique perspective at the expense of other perspectives that are incongruent and may thereby threaten or undermine the Master Narrative's authenticity and claim to the American bedrock of our nation's founding ideology: "liberty and justice for all."

In light of the Master Narrative and its legacy in and among America's other-than-WASP constituencies, our basic premise, as indicated by this chapter's title, is that a healing process is not only possible but eventual. "Eventual" because the prognosis for healing stands at a very high likelihood of being actualized; the only question is that of timing. The resilience of the human spirit bodes quite well over the final outcome that inevitably stands before us. After so much hurt and damage, the funneling of the truth about human interaction within the context and backdrop of American society will soon rise to the surface, producing a shared and collective historical consciousness. So much of this process will be determined by outgrowth and incorporation of the dynamic principles within the Collision Model.

Mutual understanding is the goal to unlocking the Master Narrative, and with the application of the Collision Model, this lofty destination can be achieved. The following keys to unlocking the Master Narrative provide practical, applicable actions that lead to shared meaning.

Key #1: Know Yourself

"Knowing yourself is the beginning of all wisdom."
Aristotle

Three circles of "self"

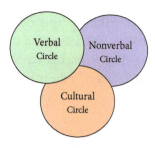

Within our highly individualistic culture, "self" is predominant. As the quote from Aristotle states and the Collision Model emphasizes, knowing yourself is the first step in understanding "other." Through having insight into one's own verbal, nonverbal, and cultural communication style, in conjunction with our historic roots, an awareness of one's identity emerges. This personal identity, when shown to the public, is the image that others see when interacting with you. Adapting that public image as our communication environment varies is necessary to be a mindful intercultural communicator. Seeking wisdom through knowing yourself is no easy task.

Key #2: Know Others

"Hurt not others in ways that you yourself would find hurtful."
Buddhist Proverb

Three circles of "other"

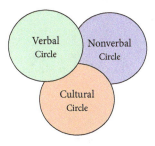

Thinking of "other" in our culture of "me" is challenging. Ironically, without others, humans cannot thrive as a species. Humans need one another. Research overwhelmingly concludes that we live longer and healthier lives when interacting with one another. Without communication, we cannot physically or emotionally survive. Thus, the second key to unlocking the Master Narrative is to reach out to others and, in the process, "hurt not others" and confirm their identity.

Confirmation: Affirming the "other" and their identity in interaction.

Disconfirmation: Communicating messages that have no value.

Acknowledging and honoring the three circles of the "other" has a profound effect on the process of understanding and its consequence of confirmation. Once this level of integrity has been mutually achieved, the interaction resonates with a form of affirmation that heretofore was missing. Being thus validated can have an enormous impact on the integrity of human interaction. This manifestation of organic validation results in trust. The presence or absence of trust between two parties is dependent on this newfound validation.

Key #3: Historical Mindfulness

"The secret of our emotions never lies in the bare object, but in the subtle relations to our own past."
George Elliott

The Collision Model

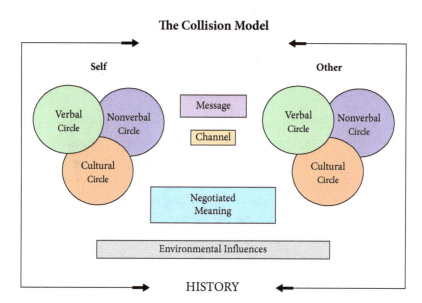

The Collision Model

At this juncture, a shared, historical consciousness, or what we call "historical mindfulness," has transpired. Such consciousness, now shared and collective, is what can truly "unlock" the Master Narrative while simultaneously administer a healing bond of mutuality, newly found and newly surfaced. This healing bond of mutuality affords what both Malcolm X and Dr. Martin Luther King Jr. referred to as the "beloved community." The Master Narrative and its effects are thus submerged beneath the new stream of a shared, historical consciousness that supersedes the confined and narrow approach to history previously adopted without scrutiny or inquiry. As a result of this "historical mindfulness," the knowledge of intercultural communication is enhanced.

Historical mindfulness provides a stream of knowledge to apply to intercultural communication for a truly mindful interaction.

Key #4: Communication Integrity

"Words—so innocent and powerless as they are, as standing in a dictionary, how potent for good and evil they become in the hands of one who knows how to combine them."
Nathaniel Hawthorne

As our chapters have revealed, each of us has unique communication patterns influenced by our history and culture. Whereas the communication style employed by the Master Narrative is stagnant in nature and nonadaptive, communication integrity involves a variation of fluid skill sets available for us to employ. Understanding which skill to use in which setting is paramount in reaching a shared meaning. What are these particular skills? In brief, the following provide *choices* for you to employ in intercultural interactions.

*__Paraphrasing__: The ability to become a mirror for the recipient in the interaction.

One of the key pathways to *mutual understanding* is paraphrasing. Paraphrasing is restating the sender's message in a nonjudgmental way, which provides a safe context in which to share.

Example:

> Jose: I'm having a tough time working this computer program.
>
> Guillermo: So, that computer program is giving you problems, ha?

In this interaction, Guillermo doesn't judge Jose for not understanding the program. His choice was to be mindful and provide support in a confusing situation. With co-cultures varying throughout the United States, becoming a mirror for each other through paraphrasing shows an inclusiveness and acceptance of "other."

***Perception checking:** Assuring accuracy in the sender's message; confirming content by verifying the sender's message, leading to shared understanding.

Assumptions are alleviated when perception checking is employed; thus, shared meaning emerges. If such steps to the perception process are violated, either intentionally or unintentionally, stereotyping can be a precurser to outright discrimination. Using the steps of perception checking provides the means to reach mutual understanding: (a) sense data, (b) interpretations, and (c) confirmation. The following scenario provides a positive outcome due to effective perception checking.

Example:

> Police officer: Sir, I noticed you're reaching for the glove compartment.
>
> (sensing the data)
>
> Is it because your paperwork is in there?
>
> (interpretation #1)
>
> Or are you reaching for something you are hiding?
>
> (interpretation #2)
>
> Can you help me here?
>
> (confirmation)
>
> Motorist: Officer, I've got my proof of insurance and title in the glove box. Here they are.

In this perception check, the police officer employed the steps in a constructive way, thus avoiding confrontational misunderstanding. What was evaded here was potential antagonism, emotional outbursts, and outright violence between the two parties.

Key #5: Listening to Bridge

"The reason why we have two ears and only one mouth is that we may listen the more and talk the less."

Zeno of Citium

Listening, although an additional communication skill, is complex in nature and lends itself to individual evaluation. While *hearing* is the biological process in which we input messages, *listening* includes the addition of a feeling component. Including a person's emotions coupled with the content of the message is what is called *active listening*.

To be an effective active listener when communicating with others, responding to each other's messages in an appropriate way is a key to understanding. Each participant has the *choice* to respond using several different listening approaches. Familiarizing yourself with these different approaches can spell the difference between success and failure when engaging with others. Your *choices* include *judging, questioning, supporting,* and *advising.* Knowing which one to use in which communication context is the key to understanding and unlocking the Master Narrative.

> **Judging:** Assigning a label to a person or a conversation; subconscious or conscious categorizaton of the message and/or the messenger:
>
> "He's obviously a racist."
>
> **Questioning:** Using interrogative methods to discover more about the message:
>
> "What happened when you were called a racist?"
>
> **Supporting:** Providing nonverbal or verbal affirmation when the participant presents a message to you:
>
> "You know you're not a racist. It's going to be OK. I'm here for you."

Advising: The receiver of the message asserts an action to be taken by the sender:

"I'd go to your coworker and ask him why he thought you were a racist."

As the Collision Model reveals, one must know the three circles of "other" to reach mutual understanding. Because a personal attempt is made to know the other's circles, choosing a method that coincides with this knowledge leads to a *mindful interaction*. For example, if a Mexican American chooses to attend a family event instead of meeting with colleagues from work, judgment statements can occur. If one understands the importance of a highly collective co-culture, then one may take a supportive approach instead. This key reminds us to choose wisely when responding to other's messages.

Listening is truly a gift we give to one another.

Key #6: Illumination of the Collision Model

"History is not a burdon on the memory but an illu-mination of the soul."
                   Lord Acton

Conclusion

In concluding this text, our discussion and review of the Collision Model as the means for unlocking the Master Narrative has been set forth. The six keys noted above encapsulate the inner dynamics of this model. This sixfold deliniation points to the critical value of unlocking the Master Narrative and reaching mutual understanding, with communication flowing both ways as displayed in the map above. In summary, below are the critical outcomes of the Collision Model:

- Honoring the history and intercultural communication styles of co-cultures within the United States
- Bridging the gaps between co-cultures
- Providing inclusiveness
- Embracing differences
- Decreasing uncertainty in interactions

COLLISION RESULTS: A new message erupts that is unique and shared only by the participants in the interaction.

The Six Keys to Unlocking the Master Narrative

1. Know yourself
2. Know others
3. Historical mindfulness
4. Communication integrity
5. Listening to bridge
6. Illumination of the Collision Model

Selected Bibliography

Adler, R., & Proctor, R., II. (2016). *Looking out, looking in.* Boston: Cengage Learning.

DeGruy, J. (2005). *Post traumatic slave syndrome: America's legacy of enduring injury and healing* (1st ed.). Portland, OR: DeGruy.

Gandy, J. O. (1998). *Communication and race: A structural perspective* (1st ed.). New York: Oxford University Press.

Gibbs, J. T. (2003). *Children of color: Psychological interventions with culturally diverse youth* (2nd ed.). San Francisco: Jossey-Bass.

Credits

CPSIA information can be obtained
at www.ICGtesting.com
Printed in the USA
FSHW022127271219
65524FS